The Fine Art of

TENNIS HUSTLING

Other Books by Rex Lardner

Downhill Lies and Other Falsehoods
The Underhanded Serve: Or How to Play Dirty Tennis
The Great Golfers
Out of the Bunker and into the Trees
The Legendary Champions
Tactics in Womens Singles, Doubles and Mixed Doubles
    (USLTA Series)
Finding and Exploiting Your Opponent's Weaknesses
    (USLTA Series)
The Complete Beginner's Guide to Tennis
Ten Heroes of the Twenties
The Lardner Report
Rex Lardner Selects the Best of Sports Fiction
Ali
Squash (with Al Malloy)
Badminton (with Frank Devlin)
Underwater Sport (with Alexander Vander Kogel)

The Fine Art of

TENNIS HUSTLING

by Rex Lardner

HAWTHORN BOOKS, INC.

PUBLISHERS / *New York*

Hawthorn Books, Inc., gratefully acknowledges permission to reprint chapter 7, which first appeared in *World Tennis Magazine.*

THE FINE ART OF TENNIS HUSTLING

Library of Congress Catalog Card Number: 75–10427

ISBN: 0–8015–2638–8

1 2 3 4 5 6 7 8 9 10

Contents

Introduction

A hustler. What is that?

By dictionary definition "to hustle" means to move fast. Therefore a hustler, if you know anything about etymology, must be someone who moves fast.

I move fast, all right, afoot and brainwise, as will be evidenced by the text that follows, which includes many of my adventures—but always with dignity.

However, the word hustler has lately taken on the connotation of beating an adversary out of something. This is achieved by conning him into a match that he is led to believe he can win and then defeating him. If the hustler is skillful enough, his opponent thinks he lost because of the breaks of the game—rub of the green, they call it in golf, and dumb luck in tennis. You generally want the fellow to come back for more. In some cases, you let him win the first time around, after which comes the big surprise.

There are golf hustlers, bowling hustlers, pool and billiard hustlers, hustlers who can inveigle you into buying drinks for them (with bar tricks, like asking you how many H's in the name of the Russian premier who banged his shoe on the table on TV); horseshoe hustlers; darts hustlers; pinball-machine hustlers; people who make crazy handicap bets, like you can't button up your vest in fifteen seconds; poker hustlers; pinochle hustlers; even balloon hustlers.

In fact, there are hustlers in every form of human activity. This would include politics, international finance, waiting on tables, giving haircuts, selling someone a brass coffin before he is even dead. And others.

Naturally, when you get to competitive sports, betting is involved. There is little satisfaction (to the hustler's way of thinking and also to the mark's) in getting an opponent overconfident or determined to defend his machismo, then whipping him by a small margin, after which triumph no money changes hands. It is like kissing your sister, as they say. For all the profit you have made, considering the wear and tear on your psyche and vocal chords, you would be better off not having played at all.

Just how you maneuver the bet is a subtle matter in tennis. In golf and in a few other sports, the betting is automatic. Golf is so weird—for example, you hit a helpless, motionless ball and are allowed fifteen minutes to judge the line of a four-foot putt and the grain of the green—that you must have something riding on every shot just to keep your interest from flagging.

A key phrase, when you think you have located a mark (and vice versa) is, "What do you say we make this interesting?"

He will give you a funny look—practiced in front of a mirror, probably.

"I mean," you explain carefully, "how about making a little wager on the match, just so we're not wasting our time."

"Like what?"

"Oh, you name it."

He considers. A quick appraisal of the opponent, who looks like he just discovered tennis three days before. "Five dollars? It's all I got with me."

"Fine. Fine. I think I can match that." And you scrounge through your pockets, finding four crumpled ones and some change.

Then you say, "Let's turn over the stake to Bill here, who's waiting for a court, and who is bonded (ha, ha), and the winner can pick up the loot later." The money is accepted by Bill.

Introduction

For one of the inflexible rules of hustling is to get the
money out and hand it over to a neutral party. It gives the
transaction a kind of official imprimatur. Besides, a hustler
does not like to be stiffed. If there was a hustlers' union there
would be a rule against it.

Then play starts. Either one of you may win the first
set—you spend most of the time judging his affluence and
gullibility, plus his greed.

If he exudes wealth, you let him win big. After the set, you
say, "Hell. I can do better than that. I'm not used to the
playing surface yet."

He favors you with a condescending smile. "Yeah," he
says, picking up and counting his winnings. "I could see you
were a class player. I was just lucky, I guess. A couple of
netcord shots that could have dropped either way. Want to
have another go at it?"

"Let me get my wind back." You puff a few times and fan
your face with your hand. "Okay. I'm ready to go. Would
you like to make it interesting again?"

"Sure." Blind optimist! He does not have any huge
amount of money, but he has just won, 6–1, playing at three-
quarter speed. But why should he have to put up any money
at all. It's like betting that a woman will sprain her ankle in
the jungle.

"For another five?" Even if by some strange quirk of fate
and the perversity of the gods who govern tennis (for such
there are), he should lose, he is no worse than even.

"Oh, I feel confident." You purse your lips thoughtfully.
"Say for a hundred."

"A hundred dollars?" (The man must be mad!) "I didn't
bring anything but a five and with your five that I won, that
makes ten." Anyway, he tells himself, where would this
seedy chap who had so much trouble finding five dollars ever
dig up a hundred? Must be a mouth bet and made
frivolously.

"Okay," he says finally. "Fine with me."

You produce your hundred—crumpled, but legal tender—say three twenties and four tens.

"If I lose would you take a check?" he asks. (Though God knows, the mark tells himself, there is no chance of his losing.)

"No." Flatly. The money goes up front and no checks.

He ponders. It's the easiest, quickest hundred he will ever make in his life. "Well, I've got it at home."

"Well, get it. I'll grab a hot dog or something."

Now the mark is "going on the send," as they say. More about this in a later chapter. Even if he has to rob a bank or pawn his wife's jewels or sell the tires on his car, he is somehow going to raise the capital.

He comes back, puffing (which is not necessarily going to be good for his classic game), and proffers the money, which Bill accepts, along with yours.

"Who serves? I guess I do," he says, eager to make the afternoon profitable.

The hustler takes his position, swaying a little from side to side, three feet inside the baseline, ready to receive.

The rest, as they say, is history.

What follows are descriptions of some of the tricks of the hustler—conning marks, luring bets, and winning against odds—along with some of my own adventures, not only as a hustler and patriot but as one of the great unrecognized tennis players of the world.

There is profit in being unrecognized.

The Fine Art of
TENNIS HUSTLING

1

A Handicap Match

When you get started talking about placing a small wager on a match, your prospective opponent naturally begins thinking about a possible edge. Something that will even out the odds, in case you are a much better tennis player than you look on the clubhouse porch or when awkwardly poking balls against an inoffensive backboard.

Sometimes it is useful, therefore, to transport odd objects that can be put to use in so-called handicap matches. For instance, I often carry around with me, as supplementary equipment, an umbrella, galoshes, leashes, flippers, a football uniform (including cleats, which does not make groundskeepers happy), a wheelbarrow that can be disassembled, and a metal bucket to wear or to hold water. (It is lighter than it looks.)

A great many players whom you meet for the first time are worried, when they compete for some kind of stake, that the pressure is going to get to them. They have visions of their wives or girl friends chiding them for dropping money that could have been spent on dinner and a movie, of their friends chortling over their defeat, and of the rabbit punch to their own ego. So they insist that you somehow limit your speed afoot, or peripheral vision, or endurance, or ability to concentrate—or all simultaneously.

In my time, I have played wearing a diving suit, a straitjacket, a suit of French armor, and a sleeping bag. If you practice for a week beforehand in these garments, you get accustomed to them—though God knows you can lose a lot of weight.

Probably the toughest match I ever played took place in Tampa in the late sixties. According to the agreement—before my opponent, the Florida state champion, would consent to risk his reputation or any of that precious green stuff—I had to wear galoshes (open), carry an umbrella, and manage five dogs on leashes. We shook on it and I opened up my equipment bag.

It was a kind of informal wager, and what was challenging about it was that I had never burdened myself with live animals before. But dogs are more manageable than tigers, I figured. We began conversing on a bench near the local courts and the talk shortly got around to money.

"But where am I going to get five dogs?" I asked the champ, a young fellow in his thirties, tanned and very intense looking. He was a hard bargainer, but I needed a hundred bucks to ransom my auto from a local garage—and winning fifty from him would just make it.

Together we set about locating five dogs, borrowing some and picking up some strays. Finally they were all fastened to leashes and I sat down, with them yapping and snarling, feeling something like Ben Hur must have when he rounded the first turn of his chariot race with Messala. A Doberman, two poodles, a Samoyed and a Russian wolfhound. A mixed bag, as they say.

A lady was practicing serves on the nearest court, while the remaining four courts were occupied by players of various sexes and abilities. My opponent, whose name was Jeff, asked the lady when we might have the court.

She didn't answer.

He got up and waved and hollered. "Hey, lady! When can we get on the court?"

"I'm practicing serves," she said without looking at him. "I've been here forty minutes and I'm going to be here another forty."

My opponent looked at me and wiped his brow. It was 125° in the shade—with no shade. Without warning the

The toughest match I ever played

Doberman gave a lunge, dragging his leash behind him, and charged toward her. She uttered a piercing shriek and started to run around the court, with the Doberman loping behind. Dobermans instinctively chase anybody who runs, which is why they are known as man's best friend. She raced toward the fence and began climbing it. She got up about seven feet, with the Doberman casually leaping up and nipping at her legs, which were drawn up under her. He backed up to make a prodigious jump and get a good piece of her as Jeff grabbed the leash and yanked it back to me. I took it in my right hand. Two of the other dogs were scratching, one was snarling, and the Samoyed went to sleep.

"Can we have the court now, lady?" Jeff called to her through cupped hands.

She nodded vigorously, still clinging to the fence.

"Hey, buddy," a slick-haired man whispered to me hoarsely from behind the bench. "How can you hold five dogs in one hand and an umbrella in the other and swing one of them bats at the same time?"

"Don't worry," I told him in a low voice. "I'll manage. If you want to make a few bucks on me, I think you can get three to two or maybe twelve to seven."

"Gotcha." He gave me a wink. "I'll put something down for you, too."

I gave him a quick nod, being otherwise occupied.

"That umbrella has got to be open," Jeff called, making his way to the other side of the court as curious spectators assembled.

"Okay." It wasn't as though I was trying to get away with something. My new friend opened it for me (a two-handed task).

"This'll shoot the odds up," he said. "And you can use it as a parasol between shots." He was off to line up persons of sporting blood. I controlled the beasts with my right hand and held the racket and umbrella in my left.

We both waived a warm-up. Jeff tossed his racket and won the serve, as so many racket tossers do from the other side of the court. He served a ball wide to my forehand and I started toward it, was yanked back by the somnolent Samoyed, was taken forward by the excited Doberman, who wanted to chase the moving ball, and tripped over the leashes attached to the other three dogs, who must have thought I was a maypole. I swung at the ball with my umbrella while toppling over, but only ticked it—15-love.

Things went along like this for a while, getting progressively worse as the dogs got more restive, the sun beat down more fiercely and the umbrella handle became more slippery. The score reached 5-love in games, with me showing a lot of trouble on my serve. It is hard to raise five dogs off the ground and make an accurate toss at the same time. I think I must have made about three points—two on Jeff's double faults and one on a net-cord shot—up to that time.

My friend with the slick hair kept apprising me of the odds: 3-1; 11-2; 20-3; 25-4; 6-1! He made dozens of bets, while Jeff and I toweled off at the net post, amidst much hilarity.

I gave my friend the office to accept anything he was offered at those odds and then changed the leashes to my left hand, the umbrella to my right, and threw away my racket, which had been an encumbrance all this time.

The crowd buzzed as I made the toss left-handed, drew the umbrella back in my right, whipped it over the ball and struck the ball with the handle. It ricocheted off the handle with terrific spin and landed in Jeff's backhand corner. A clean ace.

What followed is history, the odds plummeting as I drew even and then ahead. Jeff could not return the forehands and backhands I hit by coming over the ball and under it with the rotating ribs of the umbrella and he did not make any attempt to hit the ball on the last three points.

I unleashed the dogs to find their masters as best they might, congratulated Jeff on his fine play, collected from him and (behind the stands) from my slick-haired friend, and folded up the umbrella.

"You had me worried a little there when he had all those games on you," he said. "How did you know you could handle him?"

"You forget," I told him. "This isn't *anybody's* umbrella. This is *my* umbrella. A guy in Barcelona made it up for me. It isn't waterproof, but you sure can hit a helluva forehand with it!"

Then I ransomed my auto from the garage and set out on a hustler's tour of the nation.

2

"This Is the Hand
That Shook the Hand—"

In tennis, technically speaking, the grip is how you grip the racket. The kind of grip a player uses will generally determine the kind of shot he hits. Your experienced player (and in particular your hustler) will not look at the ball as it comes off the opponent's racket but will instead note his opponent's grip. You do not have to follow the flight of the ball at all, the choice of grip tells you where it is going.

A grip halfway up the handle means a short chopped shot. A tight grip down toward the butt means a ground stroke or lob or drop shot or smash. A loose grip on the butt means a half-volley serve (and you can claim a foot-fault if it goes in), or what we call a not-up. A not-up is when the ball has been hit short and has bounced about four times before the opponent gets to it. If your opponent is the recipient of a not-up, and he says he got it on the first bounce, be willing to concede third, but never first or second. In the meantime, recover your wind; that is the main use of this grip.

A two-handed grip means a ball over the fence, because nobody in their right mind can hit a ball with both hands on the racket.

It might seem odd, my devoting so much attention to grips in a treatise addressed to sophisticated players like you, who probably know and use at least one grip—but this section actually is not devoted to grips but rather to shaking hands.

The hand is the most important element of the grip—some experts say the *only* element; I will not argue that point here.

So you have to protect your hand—right hand if you are right-handed, left hand if you are left-handed; both hands if you are ambidextrous—or if you are one of those crazy people who holds the racket with two hands.

Since the business hand is so vital to a hustler, or to any normal tennis player, you must give it constant loving care. No heavy work, no household chores, no gardening or weed pulling, or any other activity that would develop muscles and tendons in the wrong places.

What you must watch out for particularly is how you shake hands. There is some sort of theory that holds it is manly to develop and use a firm grip for handshaking. It is supposed to show forthrightness and integrity and means you can make out with girls.

Like most theories, this is sheer nonsense. If I am going to shake hands with the president, I am not going to try to bust his hand. The same with your boss—you obviously are going to let him beat you down. The same with dukes and earls. If you break or even sprain their hands, they are either going to have you deported or frame you so that you land in gaol, sewing mailbags for the next ten years.

But a lot of people feel that there is some kind of contest of wills as well as of strength going on. Even the ladies get into the act. Some of them take you by surprise. When you extend your hand, deciding that you are not going to squeeze this little lassie's hand too hard or she will figure you for some kind of apelike bully and that will be the end of your projected romance, you suddenly find your hand caught in an inexorable vise. Your face registers shock and surprise as you feel your knuckles crack and your knees begin to buckle.

For, as far as strength in a handshake goes, there is a kind of preparation, or mental set, necessary. Let us say that you want to intimidate an opponent in this manner. For weeks you build up your grip by squeezing a rubber ball, doing fingertip push-ups, soaking your right hand in brine, working out with unsuspecting friends (whose friendships you may lose for life). I don't know if they have a special handshaking machine—they seem to have a machine for everything else, from testing golf ball pressures by socking them to throwing sucker pitches at batsmen—but if they have, you could buy one of those (estimated retail price would be about $159.65)—and practice twice a day on it.

So when your grip is strong enough for you to crack a walnut with one hand, you pick the time and site and psych yourself up: "This son of a gun is a draft-dodging pinko communist, who called a shot out on me in 1974 that was at least four inches in. Costing me a 40-15 lead in the critical fourth game of the third set. He laughs when I fall down trying to retrieve a drop shot at the net. Besides, he still owes me five dollars from a bet we made in 1967."

I remember, parenthetically, one time I was at the home of one of my wives before the happy day. Her father, whom I was not too crazy about, came home with a laborer friend. I could see instantly that the friend didn't like me—I was a tennis player and had been through high school. As we were introduced, I threw everything I had into my hand-shake—against a hand that had lifted a thousand hods and a hundred-thousand bags of cement and hammered a million nails.

Crunch! The look on his face was beautiful to see. He was strong enough to have squeezed back after the initial shock, but I disengaged. I knew, from the look on his face, that his entire life thereafter would be devoted to arranging a meeting where we could shake hands a second time.

It finally did happen, at some kind of dance eighteen months later (these things are engraved on memory). I realized that my career as a tennis player and hustler would be over if he got me good. So I gave him the most slithery, finger-jammed offering you can imagine. My hand was in the shape of a bird's beak. He tried to break at least my top knuckles, but I quickly whipped the hand back and stuck it in my pocket. He gave me a contemptuous look.

Beware of handshakes

Okay—he won the battle, but I won the war. I was able to play in a tournament the following day and eventually won it—one of the times I bet on myself. After which I jubilantly kissed the top of my middle knuckles.

So beware of handshakers. If they get you right, before the match, they can force you to change your grip, hence your stroke, and your entire game plan. If they catch you even harder, they can make you default right on the spot.

If you are serious about tennis, think hard before accepting the outstretched hand of anyone—man or woman. He/she may be trying to dominate your personality—or to bust your hand for you and gain a psychological and tactical advantage.

If you are in a position where you *must* shake hands, do as I do—do it lefty, something like Powell of the Boy Scouts. He did it lefty to lefty, but you do it lefty to righty. You have to lean over and crouch and your hand is upside down and rather helpless. But you have saved your right hand for another glorious day.

And anybody who would break your *left* hand with a manly shake—so that your service toss would be affected—is not worthy of the name of gentleman.

3

The Unkindest Cuts
of All

If you know anything about Elizabethan literature, you know that an Englishman named Christopher Marlowe wrote a popular play many years ago called *The Tragical History of Doctor Faustus.* In it, this aged necromancer and astrologer, greedy to absorb all the world's knowledge, traded his soul in to the devil. He signed a contract with an agent of the devil, the devil performed his end of the bargain, endowing Faustus with all kinds of esoteric learning (he even talked with Helen of Troy)—and then, after twenty-four years of knowing everything, time ran out.

Dr. Faustus tried to crawl out of his contract, but the devil, a stubborn fellow, would have none of it. Finally, Faustus was whisked away to hell, there to shovel coal, or whatever it was they did to keep the patrons both busy and miserable in hell at the time. Some of them probably became tennis linesmen after hell converted to shale oil.

The reason I bring this up is that when I hit a tennis ball I put an extraordinary amount of spin on it—about twelve different kinds of spin—and some of my opponents have accused me (in my presence and out of it, but I've heard about it) of having sold my soul to Mephistopheles in exchange for this skill.

When I hit the ball, and am serious about winning the point, the ball skids through the air in a strange, magical manner, changing shape and appearance. After it bounces, it changes direction and speed even more eerily. And when my opponent hits the ball with some part of his racket, it goes sideways, or pops up in the air or dribbles down into the net.

The direction the ball takes seems to defy gravity, the laws of physics, and other natural forces like the wind and the earth's rotation.

Opponents have the feeling, I realize—by their looks, gestures, and amazed ejaculations—that it is positively *immoral* to put such an infernal spin on a tennis ball. I can practically hear them saying to each other: Prince Philip would not do it; Bobby Jones would not do it; Baron von Cramm would not do it; Eleanor Roosevelt would not do it; Dr. Schweitzer would not do it.

But Hitler would do it. Savonarola would do it. Aleister Crowley would do it. M. Joseph Fouché, Napoleon's minister of police, would do it. It would be just the thing Iago would think of. To the self-righteous player, it is like pulling the king of trumps from your sleeve in bridge, putting a horseshoe in your boxing glove, leg bowling in cricket, spearing in hockey, tackling by the face mask in football, or lifting your right elbow off the table in arm wrestling.

They try, by various means, subtle and overt, to infuse the player who uses spin with massive dollops of guilt—to cure him of his ungentlemanly impulse, or, at least, to make him so uptight that he loses dignity and poise and machismo when he wins points that way.

The curious thing is that tennis is the only active sport where it is considered unsporting to put spin on a ball. Clubs will blackball you. Hooking a serve in handball so that it bounces any one of three ways is admirable. A baseball pitcher is practically required to throw a curve. Some throw curves that break inside or out or drop as they curve either way. Others develop screwballs, fork balls, and sinkers—all very effective and frequently baffling to a batter. I know I threw these tricky pitches when I had a fling at pitching as a twelve-year-old. The only ball I hurled that *didn't* spin was a three-finger knuckle ball and, because it didn't rotate, its flight was erratic. I would only use it when we were, say, twenty-five runs ahead and two men were out.

Once I caught a surprised runner off first with it—or would have if the first baseman hadn't been looking toward the plate. It is the only time in baseball history that a run was charged to the first baseman on a thrown ball intended for the batter.

Billiard and pool players take pride in the amount of English or "side" they can put on the cue ball. There is a trick-shot artist (a part-time hustler) who can put so much backspin on the cue ball that it rotates in place for twenty seconds, drilling a hole in the felt covering, and then takes of in reverse, cutting snippets out of whatever cushions it bangs into. He is now dazzling them in Uraguay.

Golfers are proud of their ability to slice and hook the ball (they call it "fade" and "draw"), and a man with a big slice is highly respected if he can put the ball out 300 yards in some direction—it does not have to land near the hole he is facing, as long as he gets distance. A chip shot is executed with backspin so that if the player misses plopping the ball into the cup it will back into it.

Silly mid-offs in cricket, placekickers, volleyball servers, ninepin bowlers, table tennis players, pinball-machine aficionados, bocci buffs—all these athletes put some kind of spin on the ball to strike the batsman (or whatever it is you do in cricket), score goals, foil the spiker, knock down pins, make a jackass out of the opponent, earn a free game or make your ball curve away from other balls. It is legal and it is approved.

Tennis, however, seems to be different. I think it has to do with its courtly tradition—where, if you were playing Henry IV, or Cardinal Richelieu, or Mme de Montespan, should you make a monkey out of His Highness or His Eminence or His Highness's mistress (especially, since she would then withhold her favors from His Excellency), you could wind up drawn and quartered or worse.

So, as a courtier or equerry or royal instructor, you refrained from putting spin on the ball, because sure as hell the bounce would fool your regal opponent and he or she might fall among the tulips and knock over the birdbath, while all the ladies-in-waiting, lord high chancellors, secretaries of state, and other spectators in attendance would burst out laughing. The only way to keep the king happy, so he would read petitions, grant boons, and let rebels like Robin Hood go free, was to hit him balls he could hit back—and then he would sign anything you liked.

Whatever the reason, there is a definite *taint* to this style of play, as I know from listening to snatches of conversation about myself when I pretend to be asleep on the clubhouse porch; or overhear a couple of parties talking on the public courts; or at a cocktail lounge or roadhouse or bar where I pretend to be sound asleep (not that I drink); or when somebody fails to hold his hand tight enough over the mouthpiece of a telephone—or when he stops up the wrong end. (Some of my tennis-player friends are not too bright when it comes to anything mechanical.) And a few conversations have been reported to me by well-meaning friends.

I am generally identified by a short biographical sketch, *sotto voce*:

"Oh, *him*." Moues, like an uplifted corner of the lips and a skyward thrust of the eyes, to indicate disapproval. "The character who hits all those d————d cuts. Between the spin he puts on the ball and the lousy shape the courts are in, you never know where the ball will bounce. And does he chortle when you miss it completely!"

"Oh, my God, Nelly, did you draw *him* for a partner? I guess we won't get a decent shot to hit. I might as well have done my curtains this morning."

"Looks like I got *him* for a partner, Jack. Try to hit all the shots to me, and tell Jerry, too. The big freeze."

On the phone at 2:32 A.M., when three indoor players are desperate for a fourth: "I hope I didn't wake you, but we'd like to have you fill in for Joe Prentice. I think it was you who busted his leg, wasn't it? (ha, ha) . . . At Luigi's Indoor Ice

Palace and Tennis Sauna. In about nine minutes, if you can make it.'' (Which involves getting dressed in immaculate white while driving the car at forty-five miles an hour and trying to remember who the players might be; what their weaknesses are; if any of them is left-handed; how high the ceiling is; if, as a guest, I am expected to bring the balls—(but all the stores were closed); if it is men's doubles or mixed, for they are two entirely different games.

In indoor tennis, God help you if you are late! Zappo! You go in and start serving.

That is because the price of a court, in prime time, anyway, is so prohibitive that only heirs, heiresses, oil sheiks, widows of brokers, or building contractors can play. Another feature of indoor tennis is that you play it only once a week (even oil sheiks cannot afford more than that), as opposed to playing outdoors four times a week in good weather. Naturally, you will want to hit four times as many shots in that one indoor engagement.

Thus, the outcast who cuts the ball as his forte is anathema to the regulars. The rallies are short, tension mounts whenever the spin artist draws back his racket, and shouts go up: ''Watch out for a cut!'' ''No, it's a slice!'' ''When it bounces, I'll yell who's going to take it!'' ''We'll *both* swing at it!'' (*sotto voce*) ''Why the hell did we ever ask this guy anyway?''

What these players of great wealth do not realize is that I have played with *kings* and have written monographs on varieties of spin—putting it on and taking it off—and the spin I impart is a very special, aristocratic type of spin. If the ball bounces erratically or ricochets off their racket in a peculiar fashion, they should be happy to have swung at it or to have hit it at all. It is like Escoffier making you a potato salad, only to have the waiter drop it as he passes through the swinging door. You didn't eat it, but Escoffier composed it. Escoffier! My God! You would be regaling your friends with the story for years.

Still another reason for relying primarily on cuts, slices, dinks, chops (severe and kindly), sidespins, underspins, and occasional topspins is (besides the amusement they afford spectators when some militant races forward in fourth gear to make a retrieve of a slyly disguised backspin drop, falls forward, and skids about three feet—"You've come a long way, baby!") that you do not have to use the big muscles. You just use what physicians call the small ones—fingers, thumb, a little wrist, maybe a little elbow—and any trainer can tell you it is less fatiguing to use the small muscles than the big ones.

That is sheer medical fact. Who do you suppose would last longer in an endurance contest—Franz von Liszt or that big Georgia boy who, huffing and puffing, lifted up one corner of the state capitol?

That is why my game is built around doing funny things to the ball. Unless I happen to be playing against royalty, a cutie on the make for me, the very rich, or have a small wager on the patsy across the net.

And after Wampahonsset, hell can't be so bad.

4

Life Is
a Great Big Tennis Court

When you are as involved with spins, cuts, and the rotation of the ball as I am, your every hand and arm action involved in the off-court process of living becomes, to some extent, a chop, or top, or slice, or sidespin shot. These fancy strokes blend in neatly with the exigencies of the real world.

For instance, when I turn a doorknob from left to right (they better not show me one that goes from right to left), that movement is the same as a topspin backhand, generally down the line. Try it. When I cut a piece of meat, drawing the knife back, it is like a delicately sliced backhand down the line, making the opponent hop an extra step in trying to reach it.

When I turn the steering wheel of an auto to the right, that is like a softly hit overspin backhand hit crosscourt at a terrific angle. You would have to race into the stands to retrieve it. When I turn it to the left, that is a forehand hit with terrific topspin, using a modified Western grip. The ball is going deep to the opponent's forehand (he being right-handed) and, when it shoots down after its forward momentum has been battered by gravity, it is going to take a terrific vertical bounce. All the opponent can do is stand with his back to the fence, leap in the air and poop it back with a kind of flat half-lob, with maybe a little underspin.

When I hammer nails (which I do as little as possible, but they say it is good therapy for someone of my volatile temperament), I am hitting short, chopped volleys from the forecourt with a tremendous amount of slice. The chop is so severe that it actually takes a divot out of the court, blades of grass and dirt explode in the air, making it difficult for an opponent to locate the ball, even if he could run forward fast enough to reach it.

On those rare occasions when I wear a hat, and on those rarer ones when I remove it (if, say, an earl's wife passes in her cabriolet and gives me a nod I am constrained to acknowledge)—well, what is closer to the flat backhand smash than that? Except the follow-through with the hat is longer. Sometimes I salute persons below the rank of earl (baronets, for instance), just to practice removing my hat, work the backhand-smash muscles and get my timing down perfect.

I seldom get into bar fights, but let us say there is an argument of an intellectual nature between me and anybody. The fellow could be a thug, a musician, somebody who thinks he knows a whole lot about politics or sports or the law or military history; he could be somebody who reminds me of a sergeant I once had or I remind him of a sergeant *he* once had (though if he was in a war, I doubt if it was the Big One)—whatever the issue, when there is an argument, certain strokes can be practiced.

I can generally absorb a lot of guff because, for me, nearly everybody is a character prancing around in a great five-act play I am directing. However, one's patience runs out sometimes. Then I draw my right arm back to my left hip, bring it up fairly fast and let the noisemaker have a rap across the jaw. What is this except a flat or topspin backhand, depending on the height of the victim? If he is of medium height, it's a flat backhand; if he's tall, it's a topspin backhand. If he should be short, it turns out to be an underspin backhand, a little like Ken Rosewall's.

If he should be terrifically tall and jamming his face down onto mine, hollering his theories about some of the above topics—"You're crazy! Where the hell did you get that information? I never heard such baloney!"—I bring my hand back and hit what amounts to a backhand lob—sky-high—imparting a little bit of topspin, because the wrist snaps forward and the knuckles turn over when I reach the top of the swing. It is the surest way I know to persuade a companion to be less dogmatic. Anyway, how often do you get a chance to practice a backhand lob with topspin, with no danger of its sailing beyond the baseline?

For about six months in my career, when I needed backhand-lob and backhand-ground-stroke practice, I spent more time in bars than out of them. (A great variety of bars, for, wherever I went, trouble seemed to follow—and innkeepers are cautious fellows, always casting eyes at the minions of the SLA.)

But if Big Bill Tilden could take a year off to rebuild his backhand, I reasoned, I could spare six months (or was it eight?) to perfect both the ground stroke and the lob. Not only did these strokes attain polish and élan, but I put on weight.

Peaceful pursuits are likewise useful. When I dial a number on the phone, that is practice for a finger-controlled, delicate-touch, forehand crosscourt drop. When I turn on the stove, that is similar to the movement of a sharp forehand chop, clearing the net by about a quarter of an inch and chewing its way through the opponent's racket strings. When I change channels on TV, which I do with alarming frequency, that is practice for a backhand drop hit at chest height. (I am sitting down at the time, dummy.)

Raising your arm in a formal toast is practice for the over-the-shoulder lob—when you have been chased back by a surprise lob hit with topspin and, because of the shooting bounce, you have no time to turn around until the point is over. Running your finger down a list of names in a phone book is fairly good practice for the overhand underspin serve, using a modified Australasian grip, and holding the racket a half inch above the butt. Not ideal, but useful.

Swatting a passing lady
simulates exactly the foreward movement
of the flat forehand ground stroke

Turning the pages of a book trains you for wristy topspin backhand drives, generally aimed down the middle to jam the opponent.

Swatting a lady (or other *espèce de royauté*) on the can as she moves by simulates exactly the forward movement of the flat forehand ground stroke, though you might be sitting down at the time.

5

The Care and Feeding of Pigeons

Naturally, when you see a mark on a bench by the court or lolling on the clubhouse porch, you do not come right out and say, "I'll play you for fifty big ones." That is overbold by any standards.

First you schmooze a little: "Nice out. Good weather for tennis. How long have those idiots been on court four? Hey, I always wanted to try a plastic racket. How is it?" (Look, but don't touch. Some players would rather have you seduce their wives than squeeze the grip: Sweat, germs, no longer virginal (or monogamous, anyway); plus all the mystic effect a strange hand might have on the sensibilities of the racket handle).

The introductions are made and the tennis reminiscences unfold, neither one of you knowing or caring if the other party is a company vice-president, a horse trainer, one of those guys who plays chess for a quarter with you (if he wins) in a penny arcade, a hangman, a bookbinder, a theologian, a gandy dancer, Judge Crater, a professional optimist, a male model (there are ugly male models), an archeologist, a Trappist monk on vacation, a genocide out on bail—or whatever. You are interested, as is he, in a narrow spectrum of accomplishments.

It turns out he was the army champion of Punjab; you once beat Prince Edward. He can be ambidextrous if he has to; you beat Rosie Casals—in horseshoe pitching (chuckle). They wanted to put up a statue of him next to Nelson's but he dissuaded them—it wouldn't have been as tall as Nelson's. He once treated Arthur Ashe and Lillian Roth to drinks in Las Vegas (both refused); you are teaching a kid, gratis (!), who will someday make Jimmy Connors's record look anemic—

Speaking of anemia, he begins.

But you get back on the track. You helped Washburn get his forehand back before he beat Wrenn during the war years; he was the fellow in the audience who shouted "Out!" and caused the brouhaha when Wills played Lenglen at Cannes. You were the chap who advised LaCoste to put an alligator instead of a hippopotamus on his shirts; he once came back to win a set when he was down, 2–4, 15–40. With Tilden as partner, you made a sacrifice bid in bridge one time and went down by only 1,540 points, whereas if the opponents had made two hearts, redoubled (Tilden was a great redoubler), the opponents would have made 20,540 points for game, set, and rubber; he once caddied (meaning acted as ball boy) for William McKinley.

"McKinley is on the ten-dollar bill, is he not?"

Thus the talk gets around to money, and a comfortable hostility is developing between hustler and hustlee—though the two have not been quite sorted out yet.

It can safely be projected that money will ride, however uneasily, on the outcome of the upcoming match. Now the general question of handicaps arises—giving points or games or both, or carrying odd things around the court, like a tray of cocktails, in the nonracket hand.

He mentions, as a kind of opening argument, some illnesses he has or had: diphtheria, dipsomania, calcification of the inner ear tubes, nymphomania, the ague, palsy, a bad football knee (but a good one remaining), epicondylitis, naturally; myopia in one eye, astigmatism in the other eye, moon blindness (he cannot drive at night when the moon is full because he is afraid he is going to turn into a wolf); some form of Asiatic arthritis that they can't even find the *bug* for, let alone a bug to send after it; diarrhea (on demand—like when he needs a twenty-minute rest); scrofula—and a bunch of other glamorous diseases that in one way or another affect his play.

When you can slip in a word edgewise, you counter with your own ailments, out of courtesy never duplicating his. These include paranoia, phthisis, endemic lead poisoning, a treacherous crick in the back, gout, one shoulder higher than the other, the same ailment Poe's Ligeia had, the ague—

"I said that," comes the sudden and startling interruption. You are not playing the game.

Sorry—but talk about allergies! To dust, to pollen, to trains passing by in the night, the news on television, people who pronounce "height" "heighth"; to windmills, Miriam Hopkins, panhandlers, potholes; to pencils whose points keep breaking when you sharpen them with the annoying result that you wind up with a stump so depleted it stays in the sharpener for somebody else to cuss; to chocolate Easter eggs . . .

And beyond all this, you are allergic to penicillin.

He will come back with a bunch of things ending in "ia" that might be diseases and might be tropical plants—because who can keep up with all the fads in diseases? You wrap the catalog up with a few of your own—fear of sharks, a little humor there—and trail off; because you have him hooked, or he has you hooked, and the idiots out on the court have played themselves into exhaustion and are vacating the premises.

"How about making it interesting?" he says, as the two of you approach the combat arena.

Now your radar antenna is up and revolving. You notice where he bought his shoes; if there are grass stains on them. If his racket has a busted string in it—though it could be wound so tight that a busted string wouldn't reduce tension, a not-unusual gambit of hustlers to induce overconfidence in opponents. If he has his bandages and braces and supports on now, or if he will put them on just before play. (A brace on the left knee means the right one is the bad one, an old football trick.) If he takes a few quick puffs of a long cigarette but controls his coughing before stepping onto the court. If he says, "Damn!" and you notice that one stem of his eyeglasses has come off in his hand. If he lays out on the bench several bottles of esoteric medicines as a hedge against falling down from apoplexy or intracardial hematoma or Santley's Disease.

Be aware, however, that all this while he will be watching *you*. Wondering about your baseball cap, your socks that don't quite match, your old basketball shoes, your racket of ancient vintage, your old and dented can with two (probably old) balls in it, your corduroy shorts; your unlit cigar, your immaculate white, long-sleeved shirt with the sleeves rolled up just beyond the elbows for freedom of movement.

The warm-up reveals a good deal, so it is better to get the preliminary betting over before it starts. Should it be per point or per game, per placement and forced error per set? Or just per set? With extra money riding on aces, double faults (you lose, naturally), number of games won in succession, and such as that.

Because it was our first encounter, we decided on something relatively simple: A bet on each game and double that amount on each set and double *that* amount on the match (two of three sets) as a whole.

"Now what would you like to, ah, wager?" I asked him, with as much insouciance as I could muster—for it is hustlers' courtesy to let the mark set the stakes. Hoist by your own petard, I think the ancient term was.

"How about five big ones?" he replied.

This gave me some pause. Five big ones. What does that mean? Could be five bucks—a reasonable wager if you are betting solely on the outcome of a match. Five bucks for an hour and a half's work—not bad. Maybe in less than an hour if he doesn't need some coddling.

He's watching *you*—in your old baseball cap,
unmatched socks, racket of ancient vintage,
unlit cigar . . .

Five big ones. Could be five fat wives that, if I won, I would have to support for the rest of my days, buying them diet pills and watching them eat candy—but that was pure fantasy. My friend was no Arab. Could be five tens—which would give anyone pause.

I did some quick calculating and figured I could lose (in the improbable event I lost) 1,080 bucks—a sum that staggered the imagination. Think of how many thousands of lessons I would have to give to young people and beginning adults; the coaxing I would have to do to keep them from becoming disconsolate over the home runs they hit; the waiting I would have to do to get onto a court; the apologies I would have to make when the pupils knocked a ball four courts down, interrupting a critical doubles match; the glowers and shrieks of agony that would ensue when I trotted down after the ball, interrupting other games on the way.

Here was another disturbing thought. When he uttered that phrase, suppose it was Damon Runyon talk. Could a big one be *one hundred dollars*? My God—the house, the car, six buckets of old tennis balls, an old chair we have out in the backyard, my trophies, my paperbacks, my canoe—all these would go down the rathole if I lost. I could imagine myself calling my wife: "Hey, listen, Martha . . . I've got some kind of bad news."

"Yeah?"

"Now don't get upset. It was something that I took a chance on and, if things had worked out the way I planned, we would have been, well . . . well, we wouldn't have had to worry about buying groceries or paying the oil bill for a couple of months."

"That would be nice."

"Yeah. Well, things don't always work out the way you want—you know? Anyway—the bad news is, I didn't come out of it as good as I expected."

"Oh?"

"Yeah. There were a couple of things I didn't figure on and I got a couple of bad breaks. Anyway, the upshot is, we don't have the house anymore."

"Well, we could sell the car and live for a while in an apartment," Martha suggested.

"That would be a good solution. But the car went, too."
Shocked silence.

"I told you I didn't have good news."

"Thank God, what little cash we have is tucked away in a savings account."

"That went with the car," I confessed.

"We could borrow on the insurance."

"I thought of that. I already did."

"*He's* got it?" she asked, her voice rising dangerously.

"Yeah . . . A bad afternoon for me . . . But I've got a lesson at four. That'll be two-fifty."

"If she shows up and if it doesn't rain and you can find a free court somewhere."

"Yeah. But it's still pretty sunny."

"Well—the coffee's on. . . . Have a good day." I thought I detected a note of resignation in Martha's voice.

(All in the imagination, of course, but you can see the depressing thoughts that sometimes hit even the most proficient hustler when, to keep the mark on a leash, he has to offer him some kind of handicap.)

Then there is always the problem, once you have him hooked, of coming up with front money—that is, put-up-or-shut-up money. Failure to pay off is known as welshing or stiffing, and you spend the rest of your days in Kansas if you do it once, and in Nova Zemblaya if you develop a reputation for it.

There are times when you are flush and times when you are busted—these affect the amount of your bet. This happened to be one of the times I was busted—successive losses at croquet, a friend balancing one broom atop another (probably fixed), riding a one-wheel bicycle all the way to the top of Spinney Hill without stopping (it was drizzling and the other guy knew it would), and naming fifty states in a minute and a half. Nebraska, where were you? Plus a few bucks thrown away to seek some kind of solace—and not getting it.

Since I was busted, I said, "Let's hit a few first and see how I feel. I got this lame shoulder from tumbling off a surfboard."

"I guess the waves must be about a foot and a half high in Manhasset Bay," he commented.

"Oh, I don't surf in Manhasset Bay," I said as he got out the balls (presumably lively), checked his pharmaceuticals and moved out to the least sunny side of the court. "This was along the Podunk River in Connecticut, with a guy in a canoe propelling me, on account of the rapids."

He turned and hit what is called a courtesy shot.

Now, in a warm-up, just like in a fencing match or chess game, you can tell a lot about your opponent's character. You can also determine stroking weaknesses and strengths and other mental and physical characteristics that will indicate how well your opponent plays. At least *I* can.

You can tell his speed afoot, his ability to go to his left or right, how he handles spin and various speeds, what his favorite shots are, if he likes to play net, if he has any confidence in his overhead, if he is an aggressive or defensive player, if he knows a few psychs (like calling "Good shot!" when you make a very ordinary shot, or cussing himself when he misses a shot nobody should even *try* for); if he is right-handed or left-handed, of course (though I know a couple of sincere hustlers who will warm up and play a set and a half righty and then switch hands after a press bet has been made. It is something not in my code, because I have practiced it and it does not work for me); the amount of clearance his balls have over the net; if he hits over the ball, or under, or sideways.

Then, when you get to the net, does he—as many determined players do—never give you anything to volley: Shots in the net ("Sorry!"), hard shots right at your tummy ("Didn't mean that!"), and lobs far over your head, some of which you have to retrieve in the grass behind the fence. "That one got away from me."

Conclusion: This gentleman is putting me on. He will give me a lead of about 4-1, then it will be hammer and tongs and, between fortuitous net-cord shots, shots off the net posts, and shots off his handle and the racket frame, he will come out of it, 7-5. I will owe him five big ones—whatever they are. To let me get even and maybe make a few bucks, he will offer to bet me (because he used up all his luck in the first set, ha and ha) *ten* big ones on the second set.

Now there are two kinds of gamblers—conservatives, like myself (generally out of necessity), and crazy ones. A crazy gambler, in my shoes, would go along and surrender the five big ones for the first set—and then offer, out of pique or a surge of self-confidence (apparently), to go for *twenty* big ones on the outcome of the second set.

This is a wise move—provided the crazy gambler is not being hustled himself; provided the mark (or hustler) wants to play a second set, greed being the ruination of many hustlers; provided an Act of God occurs, like rain—or an attendant, asking if you have a park card or some way of proving either one of you is a member of the country club whose facilities you are using, does not show his leering face.

There is nothing sadder than a hustler, beat out of hard cash because he threw the first set, racing around the island trying to find a free court so he can have a payday—and absolutely none are available. It reminds you of the scene in *The Lost Weekend* where Ray Milland walks the length of Manhattan trying to pawn his typewriter for the price of a bottle, only he happened to pick a Sunday for his hegira. There is no more touching episode in literature.

Myself, I take the money and run. Win the first set and then let the opponent do the sweating and go through the torment of making arrangements to finish the second. In a pinch—though the chances of it happening are like the odds of Woody Hayes admitting that Michigan's last-second field goal against Ohio State was really good—if I should be on the verge of losing, I know five hundred ways to stall.

Like bandaging my knee with a long wraparound bandage that falls off and needs emergency repairs—a straight pin, a safety pin, adhesive tape, a sailor's knot, a clip with teeth in it, glue, an elastic band—after every other shot; plus frequent trips to the bench for pills, gulps of water, and slugs of some mysterious medicine to keep my blood circulating—so no second set ever gets completed.

So I took it upon myself when play was about to start to ask him what he meant by a "big one."

"Fifty bucks," he said.

"So when you bet five big ones, you are betting two hundred and fifty bucks."

"I can see you got it up here," he said, tapping his forehead and then removing his sweater to reveal a right forearm the size of a grapefruit. (He still could be left-handed, having developed the right forearm through special exercises and doing nothing but hustle with the left, a lefty nowhere except on the tennis court, in the pool hall, and in the bowling alley.)

Well, it would be a new experience, anyway; and if I got in a bad jam I could pole a ball over the fence behind me and escape in the jungle while pretending to look for it, sail to Tasmania and grow a moustache and get blue contact lenses, like Shirley MacLaine for *Sayonara* (or whatever movie it was), only hers were brown because her eyes are blue and mine are brown with a little green thrown in if you look close.

So I said fine and he laid out two hundred and fifty bucks and gave me a put-up-or-shut-up look. I had fifteen dollars on me and the hustler's code is cash on the line—for his benefit more than the mark's. It means the mark has to put up front money for the privilege of losing it. Otherwise, *he* has to get the contact lenses. And the hustler is jeered at in hustler hangouts all over the globe.

What he was doing, in con man terms, was "putting me on the send." The "send" is when you have to borrow a bunch of money from relatives or casual acquaintances or sell your car or extract cash from a bank, from under your mattress, or from an old sock.

It is quite a trick, incidentally, to borrow a sum like this (even ten dollars) from a casual acquaintance. Especially when your reputation precedes you and he has seen you cross the street six times within one block so you will not have to pass certain stores or certain pedestrians on the way to your destination; plus you are approaching him with a kind of corvine look, so he can prepare a gracious refusal: "Gee, I just lent my last five bucks to Henny so he could get a new muffler." "Did you ever give me back that five I loaned you in April?" "Hey, that's funny! I was going to ask *you* for a fiver." (You can see you are going steadily downhill.)

On the other hand, my courage was bolstered by the fact that I had a sure thing—like a bet on Man o' War; or like the guy with a straight flush that he takes to the bank and uses as the basis for a thousand-dollar loan, because the guy in the pot with him keeps raising and the banker says "where's your collateral?"

So the guy says "look at this." And he shows the banker the straight flush.

"That's good enough for me," says the banker and gives him the thousand at a usurious rate of interest.

So the guy with the poker hand returns to the game and calls the other guy's bet and shows his hand and wins the pot. Another ending is—he had an ace-high straight and lost to the other guy's full house. Another is, the opponent had a higher straight flush—to the queen, say.

Personally, I prefer the version where he wins the pot,

plays it cozy for the rest of the evening, stiffs the bank and skips out of town. You may see why in a moment.

Accordingly, playing it by ear, I told my pigeon to practice serves for about fifteen minutes, and I would be back with the scratch by then. I hied me to a bank, disregarding a few acquaintances who crossed the street when I approached them.

No customers were in the zoo, as they call the fenced-off section in fiduciary circles, so I entered, sat down opposite a neat man in a blue serge suit, and mentioned my business.

"What is your collateral?" he inquired.

I showed him my good right arm.

"You're a mugger?" he asked, raising his eyebrows. (I'm sure a mugger would have been considered a better risk than, say, a short-story writer.)

"A tennis player," I said. "'I have me a pigeon and I will have your money safely back to you in a little over an hour."

He called the manager over. The manager said it was a good investment and I could have the money on the spot, provided I got two bonded cosigners who owned their own homes or the apartment houses they lived in.

There was not time—and not the slightest chance—that I could do this, so I thanked him profusely for his courtesy, energy, and parsimony and exited to the busy thoroughfare to seek a loan shark I know, by the name of Joey. He is out of Damon Runyon by Frank Nitti and dresses like a procurer would if he had the last twelve lady Oscar-winners in his stable, all shot full of expensive booze and Spanish fly. That is the impression he gives with his shooting cuffs, the crease in his checked trousers, the mirror shine on his high-heel stompers and the stylish slant of his snap-brim fedora. He oozes wealth and success and suburban depravity. A figure to be envied.

He was standing by the library steps near our imitation plastic lion. I came up to him and said, "Joey, I need two hundred and fifty big ones."

"How come you're in your underwear?" he asked, trying to figure out why I needed a sum that size.

"I got me a pigeon," I said. "I need it for upfront money to hype the scam before the blowoff."

"I think the pigeon's got *you*," he said. "Do you know you could get busted on a 1270A and a 1735?" He knew the felony statute numbers better than a harness bull.

"I am about to play tennis," I told him. "This is the proper formal tennis costume."

"What have you got in the way of collateral?" he wanted to know.

"I went through this at the bank," I said wearily, showing him my good right arm.

"I'm surprised the bank guard didn't hold you for the cops," he said. "A clear case of attempted fraud and embezzlement." He laughed in his sinister way. Then he led me into an alley and peeled off two hundred and fifty big ones, and I pocketed it. "I guess you know payday is Monday, at the usual six for five."

"You'll get it," I said. "Thanks a heap, Joey."

"Always nice to deal with you guys," he said in parting. "Puts us solidly in the real estate business."

Hurrying back to the court, I found my opponent chatting with a buddy of mine named Fred on the bench by the court, which was empty. He got up, a little impatiently, when I approached.

"I got the moola," I told him.

"Where did you have to go for it?" he demanded. "Baluchistan? You've been gone forty minutes."

"Well, your serve should be pretty sharp from all that practice," I said amenably. (Though God knows he did not look fatigued.) "You'll understand if I want to warm up a little." I produced my half of the bet. "Fred here looks honest." (Good-natured chuckle.) "He can hold the stakes."

Fred was willing; one or both of us competitors might have a seizure on the court and conceivably the money would somehow be forgotten in the confusion. Though I seriously doubted it.

We started hitting back and forth, me testing him with cuts and chops, now that the contest was official, he testing me with tops and, as behooved one of his years, with "nothing" balls.

He tossed his racket for serve and won it. Then he started play—ignoring the first-serve-in rule, which should have aroused my suspicions.

Arthritis! Rheumatiz! Dengue fever! The man was the healthiest specimen I ever laid eyes on. His serve came in like a bullet from a Mauser. Fifteen–love. Thirty–love. I got my racket on a ball by swinging while he was raising his left hand to toss it into the air. It caromed off the frame. Forty–love. Shades of Heffernan, Zammer, and Gonzalez! The best I could get out of this, I figured, was a tie. He served a ball in the net. Maybe the second serve is returnable, I thought.

Not by me. It started for my forehand, curved in the air to my backhand, bounced and spun like a Frisbee at a right angle to my left. Rather than bother the doubles players on the next court, I let it zip by for an ace.

We changed courts. "That's an effective serve you have there." It does no harm to be friendly.

He looked disconsolate. "I'm not getting my wrist into the shot," he announced. He moved it back and forth experimentally.

What is the fare to Fiji? I wondered. Do their airlines take credit cards? And could I somehow get a credit card before Monday?

I invoked the first-serve-in rule. He had heard of it and agreed to the provisions. A thought crossed my mind: If I could just keep serving faults from, say, 3:30 to 7:30, at which hour it would get dark, time would run out and the match would remain unfinished. But could anyone serve for four straight hours? In addition, there was always the risk that a stray ball might land in the deuce court and that would be the end of this particular gambit. After that, out serves are called out and play is continuous.

But I was determined to win the point, so I kept serving flat with a little sidespin to his backhand and finally he went after one (probably growing impatient) and netted it. Most receivers, in order not to dig holes in the right side of the court, are willing to sacrifice the first point of the opponent's first service game.

Then he started putting away his returns, off both sides and in the middle. I have an immense repertory of serves: Overhand, sidearm, wristy, classic, slice, flat-slice, flat-underspin, American twist, underhand, backhand. He got my best ones back, with authority. He followed that by winning his own serve at love. Thus far, you might say I had lost a hundred and twenty-five dollars, the set being half over.

Then a ball disappeared. He was chasing a ball from another court that had bounded onto ours and I knew I had two in my hand to serve with, but one kind of slid inside my shirt and I picked up the one behind me to make two. I lost a couple of points—it was beginning to get hairy—while we searched in vain for the missing ball. He even wandered down the battery of courts and minutely examined the balls of other players.

When he came back, I gave him some bad news. There is a kind of sewer behind one of the courts, for drainage purposes, and another of our balls had dribbled down it and was now floating in the East River somewhere.

"My God!" he said. "We can fly to the moon, but you can't put a screen over that damn drain?"

"There's a committee working on it," I told him. "But the chairperson got herself knocked up and is expecting a bouncing baby. . . . Anyway, there's one ball left. We can finish out the set with that. I've played competitive tennis in bars—all hypothetical and fantasized, of course—with no balls at all."

"That's the way you always play," some friend muttered, with a savage smile, as he passed by to round up a doubles game. "Them goddam cuts that twist every which way."

"Okay, serve," my opponent said.

I did. A fault, a heated return. The second ball was in and he skewered it with a down-the-line forehand that I barely touched with my racket. I lofted it far over the fence behind him and into a grove of poison ivy and poison sumac surrounded by white-on-black warning signs.

"Sometimes I wonder if we really reached the moon at all," I mused aloud. "Maybe it was all some kind of gigantic hoax to promote the sale of right-handed golf clubs."

He glowered in my general direction. "I guess that winds up the match," I commiserated. "It would have been a corker." He approached the net in a state of near-shock, having probably been forced to release his fantasies of how he would spend my money like a flock of wild cormorants.

"Maybe we could get up a doubles game, the opponents furnishing the balls," I suggested.

He glared at me.

"Maybe we could get a small wager down."

He brightened at that and nodded glumly. But (as I suspected), once bit, twice shy. We met seven refusals in a row.

"The guy who cuts everything." My reputation preceded me.

"Can we buy some tennis balls somewhere?" he asked. "I would go halvies with you, and the winner keeps the balls."

"I'm afraid I don't have time," I told him. "I've got a lesson in twenty minutes."

"You take lessons?" He acted surprised.

"I *give* them."

"You—oh, my God!" He doubled over and started to laugh and wheeze and carry on like a man demented. He staggered over to the bench, bent over and clutched his stomach. It was an ailment he hadn't bothered to mention.

"Fred," I said to the stakeholder, "return our money. The match was inconclusive."

Fred complied in a solemn way. Without bothering to count the bills, I bade my hysterical friend farewell, said I hoped we could have another contest sometime, showered, slipped into some casual clothes and strolled down the street.

I had two hundred and sixty-five dollars in my pocket, which makes any party expansive. Some acquaintances passed by and, noting my benign expression, did not bother to cross the street. On the other hand, my expression was not so benign that they could anticipate getting a loan paid back. A cozy bar beckoned.

I slid through the door, planted myself at the bar and removed the tennis ball from inside my shirt, where it had begun to itch, and started squeezing it for the benefit of my finger muscles. I ordered a shot of something with a kick to it.

After a quick belt or two I looked around. The bar was half full—a bunch of dark male shapes, arguing, chuckling, brooding, solving international problems, telling lies.

I selected a medium-sized, brooding fellow. "Do you play bar tennis?" I asked him, referring to a game played with only one's wits and knowledge of tactics and strategy.

He nodded, a little bleary-eyed.

"For a shot and a chaser," I said. He was willing.

Was there such as thing as a bar tennis hustler? Hardly likely.

"I'll serve," I said, swigging down a rye-on-rocks, followed by a great draught of English ale to lubricate my thinking muscles.

Clearing his throat, he put the ball in play. "An American Twist to the backhand, well-disguised, that kicks high to the receiver's left with such spin that you have to hit it sideways if you want it to flutter towards the net. The rear service linesman makes not a peep, so you know it has got to be good."

"I know nothing of the sort," he asserted. "I have had problems with this linesperson before. He has double vision, which is not the most fortuitous characteristic in a linesfellow. I appeal the call, and the umpire, well aware of his optometric trauma, will request that you play a let."

I could see I was in big trouble and ordered a double. But it looked like a pleasant and challenging ending to what could have been a disastrous afternoon.

I took a patient breath, studied his position closely and put the ball in play a second time. "A slice serve with reverse spin, like Hubbell's screwball, sharply angled deep to the forehand corner..."

A little later on I would reveal to all and sundry that I was a lefty.

6

The Hustler as Teacher

For one reason or another, it is not always possible to make a good living by hustling bets based on your tennis ability. Sometimes you overextend yourself; sometimes you find you are the hustlee; sometimes money is tight. So you have to supplement your income by teaching—a profession that can be very tough on the nerves.

Teaching pupils in the difficult art and science of tennis gives rise to a whole bunch of problems (such as scraping them up in the first place), but eventually you find ways of solving most of the problems, and you can earn enough to buy gasoline, especially in foul weather.

I personally would rather play in unfavorable weather than when it is sunny and mild. In the first place, you do not have trouble getting on a court. When winter winds blow and snow descends in fluffy white cakes, and ice forms spontaneously on the sidewalks; when everybody else is huddled by a fire or, if they are wealthy enough, playing tennis indoors, or in Florida watching the dogs run.

In the second place, you have recourse to all kinds of excuses when you miss a shot or (more important) when your pupil misses a shot—the ball did not bounce because it landed in a puddle and floated away, or a blast of wind blew it sideways across the court, or it skidded on the ice, or the rain made the fuzz so heavy it cut through your racket strings.

Often you will find, when you have scheduled an outdoor lesson in January, February, or March, the pupil or one of his alarmed parents will phone and suggest the lesson be postponed for any one of several reasons: Snow covers the court; a gale is blowing; the rain is coming down in diagonal torrents; the sea has ripped away all the piers—or some such nonsense as that.

In such exigencies, snow can always be shoveled off a court before play; puddles can be swept away and blotted up with old newspapers. Cold blasts from the north ice cap may be blowing hard where the pupil is, but it is a windless, cloudless day out on the courts.

A parent calls up and hollers into the phone, "You'll have to cancel! It's raining like hell here!"

"Well," you assure him calmly, "it's not even *drizzling* here."

When the pupil shows up, a glum figure wearing a raincoat and rubbers, blowing on his hands, his racket carefully encased and snuggled underneath his raincoat, he is surprised to see you dressed in summery slacks and a light sweater—outfitted for a tennis game in a Polynesian climate. Beneath the clothing you naturally wear three suits of thermal underwear and may have fortified yourself against the chill with a few belts of bonded stuff—but he has no suspicions about such artifices.

Never, while instructing, do you complain about the cold or wind or ice or the sepulchral gloom, or balls drifting downstream instead of bouncing. When the pupil complains, you merely nod casually and send him a succession of balls to swing at.

You also make light of the rampaging elements and chilly temperature: "A little rain never hurt anybody." "I'm surprised there aren't more people out playing on an invigorating day like this." "Rain water is supposed to be good for your hair. They bottle it in Oswego." "A breeze like this forces you to concentrate." "When you hit against the wind, you develop a powerful squint." "You sure can't complain about the sun getting in your eyes." "A little hail never hurt anybody." "Playing in subzero weather is the best way to avoid colds."

One thing an instructor must remember to do, in good weather and bad, is to keep making noises. If you and a pupil are merely hitting balls back and forth across the net, with no instructions being offered, he will start thinking: What am I paying this egg for? I could be hitting against a wall for nothing or with some cutie and maybe get her drunk later.

So it behooves the instructor to holler, "Nice shot!" whenever the pupil hits a ball over the net. Along with "That's the way!" "Peach!" and "Aiiiii-yah!" when he hits one you have to stretch to reach. The more varied the complimentary phrases in his vocabulary (I have about eighty, so I never have to repeat one during an hour-long lesson), the more sincere he sounds and the more likely the pupil is to come back for another lesson.

When the pupil misses a shot—and he will—it behooves the instructor to suggest a correction. If the ball lands in the net—"Hit it higher" (and demonstrate). If it sails over the fence—"Good stroke—but try to keep the return in the vicinity of the court." If he misses the ball entirely and loses his racket—"Good footwork on that one—but try to hit the ball at waist height."

Should you, the instructor, inadvertently hit the ball over the fence, you chuckle and say, "I thought I'd experiment with that grip you've been using on the forehand. I think I see what you're doing wrong. The thumb should be *around* the handle—not on the same side as the fingers."

One thing you should avoid is telling the pupil something like, "Today I think we'll concentrate on the backhand." There are good reasons. Suppose that, because of a hangover or bad luck or a gale blowing the wrong way, you simply cannot hit a ball to the pupil's backhand. He will start giving you funny looks. Then you have a choice of saying, "My

God, all this time I thought you were left-handed!'' or ''Meanwhile, it would be a mistake to let the forehand get rusty.'' It is also a mistake to keep hollering ''Whoops!'' every time you send a ball to the wrong side, or your pupil will start thinking about asking for lower rates.

So it is better to tell the pupil you are going to practice something *general,* like hitting the ball off the front foot or the back foot, and then see where your shots are heading. If conditions are absolutely disastrous—you cannot return a ball over the net and the pupil is beginning to stare in bewilderment—you had better immediately start him practicing serves. Or learning a new one. You can either yell instructions while standing behind the baseline—''Toss the ball higher!'' ''Bring the racket back sooner!'' ''Face more sideways!'' ''Try to hit the ball on the strings!''—or stand behind him on his side of the court and keep changing his stance, grip, backswing, forward swing, weight shift, pivot, and so on.

After giving him each new piece of advice, you carefully watch his moves while he hits six balls. If any of them goes over the net, you are lavish in your praise. But for the love of God, never demonstrate the serve yourself! You may miss the ball entirely—to explain which you have to be extremely glib—or fail in successive attempts to place the ball in the little box. You know you have lost a pupil when he casually remarks, ''Maybe *I* should be giving *you* lessons.''

Do not come equipped with too many balls. About ten is the maximum. For one thing, if they are scattered all over the court, your pupil may clumsily trip over one and bust his ankle. Not only is the rest of the lesson shot (he is certainly going to prorate the amount he owes you), but he may be laid up for a couple of weeks. (Maybe you can visit him and teach him tactics, but I doubt it.)

Also, after you have exhausted your supply of balls in a rally, you and the pupil must consume a certain amount of time in gathering them up and replacing them in your bucket.

This is time that registers on the clock. However, you do not have to chase down wildly errant shots or dream up flowery compliments for the pupil. It is a period of relaxation. If you are clever you can extend the time by getting your pupil to talk about his school work, or business, or operation, or some TV show he saw, and the minutes will fly by.

Naturally, a teaching hustler does not dress anywhere near the same as a playing hustler. The latter tries to look like a person who has never held a racket in his hand before, is ignorant of all the traditions and courtesies of the game and, in fact, has suffered some kind of mysterious brain damage which affects his concentration and coordination; in short, somebody whom nearly anyone with two arms and legs, a knowledge of the rules and a reasonable killer instinct could beat.

This can be done partly by the choice of clothing (I have earlier described one of my outfits) and by wearing a slack-jawed, vacant-eyed expression which brings out the vulpine character of prospective opponents. Many of my friends, I now reflect, could have made great hustlers had they not become lawyers, doctors, conductors, embezzlers, inventors, or ferryboat captains. They certainly have the physiognomical equipment for it.

No, your teaching hustler must look like Mr. Tennis, his knowledge of the game reflected in his choice of equipment and the smart casualness of his adornment. Apparelwise, he should look every inch the compleat player: Wearing a relaxed shirt in contrasting colors, made of 50 percent polyester and 85 percent orlon acrylic, with a three-button placket front, checkerboard squares running in broad bands across the chest and stomach, and interspersed with tiny representations of wooden rackets on the side vents; off-white straight-legged flannel trousers, which drape over the instep, slash side pockets and twin hip pockets large enough to transport three balls, a rubberized waistband that can be let out for purposes of breathing, crossed tennis rackets on the hips and side-leg vents with personalized initials on them in fluorescent orange; a long-sleeved V-neck sweater in eggshell and fuchsia with contrast stitching in red and brown, made of 83 percent blended soft cotton and 3 percent acrylic nylon, with a snap closure that can be let out and bright green patch pockets, which can be removed with scissors for dry cleaning; supersocks of machine-washable soy cloth in maroon and blue stripes set off with see-through pompons; coal-black basketball shoes for a better grip, made of 58 percent canvas and 43 percent Jakartan rubber, and off-white laces with a few knots in them. Plus essential accessories like dark glasses, matching wristbands, a headband in clashing colors, a mechanical scorer, which cheats a little bit, a towel with the words "Hilton Head" emblazoned on it in purple; and, of course, six tennis rackets, which need not be of the same make or generation.

Thus clad, if you are careful not to be placed in the position of having to hit too many balls to your pupils, you can enjoy many years as a successful teaching-pro hustler.

7

Calling 'Em
as They See 'Em

It is interesting to note that there is no such thing as a *pure* tennis player. Nobody who plays tennis has done nothing but play tennis. Tennis players are brokers, doctors, insurance salesmen, carpenters, cashiers, millionaires, token-collectors, doormen, steeplejacks, masons, truck drivers, jewelers, lifeguards, psychiatrists, TV repairmen (I love to get *them* on a court!), homemakers, masseuses, piano-tuners, bartenders, roof repairers, merchant seamen, dukes, and so on.

You probably get the point. Tennis is not the be-all and end-all of their lives. Though God knows you might think it was, sometimes, when they are arguing strenuously about where a ball landed, even though it is not going to change the international situation or get us to Jupiter. Or when they buy fancy equipment, as though, by some magical whoop-de-do, it is going to improve their game. Or being ecstatic for weeks (despite being indicted for embezzlement) over beating some poor shnook, 6–3, 6–1. Six-one! They are like Roland relating the defeat of the Moors.

It has been my observation that, curiously, the members of each specialty and profession have their own special vocabularies and argots when reporting a tennis fact (or fancy). Like a ball hitting the net tape on a serve and then trickling over; like complaining about an opponent's flagrant foot-fault; like instructing a doubles partner to damn well cover his alley.

Here is how they notify the opponent, or opponents, that a shot he, or they, hit, landed out:

Meteorologist: "There's a fifteen percent chance that your shot was in."

Actor: "Out! Out! See the damned spot?"

Engineer: "The ball might have looked in, all right. But the line is crooked at that point. So technically it was out."

Fiancé: "Darling, have I ever lied to you?"

Casting Director: "Very impressive. I'll let you know."

Assistant D.A.: "Okay, fella. We know the ball was out. I happen to have two witnesses who will swear it was out. Now let's have your side of the story. You're aware of your rights?"

Psychiatrist: "Just take your time and tell me how the shot looked to *you*."

Adman: "I'm only noodling, you understand, but I think we should drop our opinions on this down the well and see if they splash. How does that strike you as a tentative, off-the-top-of-the-head suggestion, George?"

Astrologer: "This is probably not a propitious day for you to try to hit down-the-line forehands, since Jupiter is in the House of Virgo."

Tax Auditor: "I'm afraid I'll simply have to call the shot out unless you can back up your claim with some sort of concrete evidence—a couple of bonded witnesses, a clearly defined mark on the court, film from an instant-replay machine or something of that nature."

Linotype Operator: "Outetaoinshrdlu mrf mrf mrf."

Horseplayer: "The shot was good up to the last split second, then it kind of came on a little too fast and rose a little and by that time the line rushed by and there's nothing to do but call it out by a sixteenth of a furlong and hope for better luck with the next one. But it was one hell of a try, you know what I mean? That kind of luck can't last forever."

Politician: "This is a decision I've given some deep thought to and, frankly, I called it out. Maybe it was in and maybe it was out; nobody can be absolutely certain about these things, all factors considered. Your position may be that it was in. Now, why don't we do this, so everyone will be satisfied: We'll call your shot in, so your side is satisfied, and I'll take the point, which is all I care about, anyway."

Philologist: " 'Out,' adverb, from Middle English *ut, oute,* from Anglo-Saxon *ut.*"

Hipster: "Man, the yellow one looked out and the square green one looked in and the wavy polka dot one hasn't come down yet. Take seven-and-a-half points, like. Hey, which one of us is serving?"

Optometrist: "There happen to be two lines here and I believe the ball hit outside both of them."

Judge: "Young man, I'm not sure I like the look you're giving me. I might call the next two shots out also."

Magazine Editor: "The feeling here was, I'm sorry to say, that the shot was not quite good enough to make the grade. But thanks anyway for a very fine try."

Movie Producer: "Jack, I have news for you."

Doctor: "Sorry, but I don't call down-the-line shots. But I'll give you the name of someone who does. And, if necessary, he'll be able to furnish you the name of a specialist who calls them on the backhand side—when they're hit with a metal racket. On indoor clay. Pay the receptionist on the way out."

Geologist: "Remarkable how the ball indented the shale-conglomerate-sandstone substratum about three centimeters beyond the line here. Come over and take a look at it before you serve the second ball."

Radio Announcer: "A very exciting and dramatic decision coming up."

Dentist: "This might hurt a little bit."

Attorney: "I don't wish to upset you, but frankly . . ."

Garage Mechanic: "I would say, roughly, everything

considered, that the ball was approximately two feet in. But you'll have to come back later for a more accurate estimate. It could have been out.''

Night-club Bouncer: "I think you just made a big mistake, buddy.''

Loan Consultant: "Sorry.''

Artillery Spotter: "The direction was perfect, but the elevation was 3.6 degrees too high.''

Chess Expert: "Hmmmmmm . . . Are you sure you wanted to do that?''

Diplomat: "At this particular juncture, I'm unable to say anything conclusive about it, one way or the other. But I can tell you, in all candor, that a ball was definitely hit. Absolutely and unequivocally no doubt about it and you may quote me. As to determining whether it landed in or out, or somewhere in between, or who precisely bears the responsibility for whatever action it may have taken, or did not take—well, we will have to await further developments. No, don't say that. Perhaps I'd better consult with my partner and if no progress is made from that discussion, we will very likely approach the net and confront our opponents, establishing a deténte, as it were, before announcing either a temporary or permanent decision. If you quote me, kindly use the term 'a backcourt spokesman.' ''

Honeymooner: "Lovely shot! What grace! What exquisite form! But serve the next ball.''

Metaphysician: "The shot appeared out from my vantage point as a Berkeleyan realist, but I gather from your dubious countenance that you saw it differently. Until we gather more data, let's each accept fifteen points.''

First Sergeant: "The ¢x%#&**!!! thing was out! What are you—some kind of *¢&*§*!! guardhouse lawyer? You missed the #*¢%§!! line. Serve the &*¢&*§*!! ball, you dumb stupid ¢&#*#&%! yardbird!''

Film Director: "Terrific! What a sweetheart! But let's do it just once more for protection.''

Barfly: "Jim, how about serving me one more? For the road."

Plumber: "Oh, brother—are *you* in trouble! You need a new racket, new shoes, new glasses, and a complete overhaul of your Australian hat. Unless maybe you're looking forward to an explosion."

TV Emcee: "Oh, I'm so sorry! You missed and you don't win the point! That's too bad! But maybe you'll get the next one. Aren't we having scads of fun?"

TV Repairman: "Now, don't be alarmed, but what you need is a special set of low-tension transdigitator polygonic strings, which are made only in a little town outside Milwaukee."

Self: "Out. Tough. If you don't like the heat, stay out of the kitchen."

8

Playing with a Hangover

Sometimes, as occasionally happens to all of us, you find you have to roust yourself out of bed at eight, or ten, or twelve in the morning on a weekend and somehow make it over to the court for an important doubles match—when you have a hangover.

I don't mean an ordinary hangover; I mean a *raging* hangover, with all the classic symptoms: Pounding head, lack of balance, eyes that don't quite focus, a tongue that feels like wet carpet, a queasy stomach, sweats and chills alternately, the shakes in both hands, a kind of tic in the left cheek, a throat that wonders what has been happening to it, lungs that are ready to pack up and quit, aches over various unknown parts of the body. Plus, in this case, bruises and scratches of unknown origin; a sense of doom, probably justified; and barrels of guilt—a black, sticky substance when not regarded in the abstract.

You look out the window, hoping for rain, hail, or a squall, so you can't play outdoors. A blizzard, hurricane, or earthquake, so it's impossible to even get to an indoor court to play. Tough luck. It's a beautiful day, with the sun beaming down, the birds expressing their territorial imperative, kids screaming by on their motorbikes (one of the dubious benefits of a bad hangover is that your hearing improves to a remarkable degree), the man next door hammering on his boat. If only Thor would hurl down one of his thunderbolts and destroy this entire block it would solve a lot of problems.

At this point, you have several choices: Roll over and forget the whole thing; call up one of the other players and say you are sick—you are actually dying—and recommend they find a last-minute substitute. . .

None of these remedies lies in the escape repertory of an honorable man. What remains, provided no happy cataclysm occurs, is to disentangle yourself from the covers, throw yourself into a state of Transcendental Meditation and stagger into the breach.

Now what—you try to recall as tiny land mines explode inside your head—are the classic hangover remedies? They must be legion—different in different lands, different for different personality types, and as ancient as Job's walking stick:

Hair of the dog. Worcestershire and raw egg. Steam bath. Hold potato peelings over your forehead and think beautiful thoughts. A great big meal, with all the fixin's. Wing of bat. Ear of toad. Sleep for eighteen hours straight (impractical in this case). A raw carrot in cremé de menthe. A bath in ice cubes with a hot water bag on your brow. A Bloody Mary without the tomato. A raw onion sandwich on pumpernickel . . .

None of them seems to work—at least those you have any stomach for trying. So there's nothing to do but slowly, painfully get dressed—between great draughts of life-preserving water, get picked up by an ebullient member of the foursome (who got there despite your prayers), and race over to the court, while he chats amiably and endlessly about his pet rabbits.

A point I would like to make, parenthetically, is that, for psychological reasons, you do not tell your partner—or your opponent—about your flaming hangover before you play. (Afterwards, okay. Win or lose, it makes you a hero.) But no one feels another's pain. You'll receive no sympathy. But you do give your opposition an immense tactical advantage, because they know that, under the pressure they can apply, you will crack like a four-day-old egg. Your partner will be your enemy for life if your side loses, knowing all the while the real reason your side is sliding down the chute.

One of the best things to do when you are playing tennis with a hangover is to stall. It is a distinct science—in some favored few it is an accomplished art—and in the following pages I will reveal some of the arcane tricks of the trade.

Stalling, in some respects, is reminiscent of Horatio at the bridge; Washington's retreat from the British on Long Island; Johnston holding out against Sherman at Atlanta; Korsakov falling back from Napoleon's grenadiers before Moscow. . . . Give away land for time. This allusion may be not quite applicable to tennis, but here is what I am getting at:

If you stall, you will not use up precious energy and may survive the day; if it is done subtly and efficiently, stalling may cause your foes to lose their poise and tempers and thus throw themselves off their game. If your team is losing, your delaying tactics may prevent the match from ever being finished—because time will have run out (other players will swarm onto the court, making continuation impossible). (Or a storm may blow up or a mad bull will run across the court, affecting the bounce, or you will be called to the colors.)

Now, stalling is not only a valuable tool for the player suffering from the world's worst hangover. It is a useful tactic to employ when you are dog-tired; when you are getting your can beat off by a superior opponent; when you adjudge your opponent to be one of those hyperactive types who likes to keep his momentum going; when you are far off your game and need time to sort out the reasons for it.

If you are a hustler and losing (and don't wish to lose, for monetary reasons), the art of the stall has simply got to be in your repertory (along with an expression of surprise when a close shot of yours is called out and with a fake display of temper now and then to make your opponent think you are coming apart at the seams).

Here are some ordinary stalling tactics with which every player is probably familiar—indeed, may have used at one time or another:

Wiping off one's glasses after every point, seeing if the lenses are clear, finding they are not and continuing to wipe until the outraged opponent is constrained to cry, "For God's sake, man! You'll wear the glass out! Here. Take mine."

The person who wears contact lenses (and even one who doesn't) can abruptly stop play in the middle of a rally—especially on a shot he cannot reach—and blurt, "My God! My contact lens popped out!"

Then begins a search by both players on their hands and knees—maybe enlisting the help of some Samaritans on the next court—to try to spot the elusive, nearly invisible thing. Locating a contact lens on a surface as large as half a tennis court is nearly impossible and, after about twenty minutes, the opponent will realize this.

He rises and says, "Well?"

The lens-wearer thrusts himself to his feet and says, "Ah, the hell with it. I'll play without the lens."

He has achieved his purpose. He has regained his breath, or stopped his opponent's momentum, or killed so much time that the match cannot possibly be completed. Besides that, when play continues, the victim of the hoax will probably be so outraged or bewildered that he will hit every ball as hard as nature allows and very likely will snap something before the match is finished. Maybe his mind.

Another interesting ploy to use to drive an opponent mad is to give him the Bounce routine. The Bounce is employed by you when it is your turn to serve—but you don't serve. Instead of tossing the ball in the air, you bounce it near your left foot. You catch it and bounce it again—as slowly or as rapidly as your skill permits. (I conduct classes in this specialty.) The receiver, swaying back and forth, twirling his racket, ready to hop in the air and dart to his left or right, starts counting after the fifteenth bounce.

Then he starts thinking about the time element. It takes half a second to bounce a ball and catch it; there is a quarter-second pause and then another bounce. Pretty soon the stars will come out or the next group to play (indoors) will arrive. What if the receiver says, "I concede the point. Let's move to the next court"? What guarantee has he that the bounce specialist will not start again over there? None at all.

Eventually, though, the bounce specialist, out of courtesy, will serve the ball. It also gets tiresome, even for a compulsive winner, to bounce a ball half the time he is on the court, ostensibly to derive enjoyment from competition and exercise.

There are mighty few receivers, after facing a vertical bouncing ball for ten minutes, who can hit one moving horizontally. So the bouncer is almost as sure of winning the point as the server is when the first-serve-in rule is invoked.

(I should mention that not all bouncers are that skillful. Sometimes you run into one with the habit pattern, or tradition, of bouncing twenty-four times, then winding up and serving. But if he should miss the ball—if it hits his foot, or takes a *bad* bounce, or his fingers wear out—and it rolls away, he is psychologically compelled to start over at "one" again. The difficulty with this technique for stalling and driving your opponent crazy is that, because of where your eyes are focused, you cannot spot him if he should sidle up to you and deliver a crashing blow with his racket to your left wrist or right knee. Then it is up to the umpire to determine which of you should default.)

Impulsively deciding to measure the net is another way to delay the game, when that seems to your advantage. After you have lost a tough point, you stroll forward and measure the net (using a racket with an extra-long handle).

"Too high," you announce.

Your opponent, a suspicious bird, will naturally check. But the evidence is irrefutable. Since it was you who discovered the error, it is up to him to correct it. That is simple mathematics. He, therefore, repairs to the crank and, while you holler instructions and raise or hold down the wire supporting the net, he pulls the crank back or edges it forward—and pretty soon it is going to snap back on him (a law of physics). To keep from breaking both thumbs at that critical point, he is going to have to release it quickly. Naturally, the net sinks in the center, like a deflated barrage balloon. And that is the abrupt end of the set—unfinished and unsung.

A more simple way to delay the game is to pick up a foreign ball that rolls onto your court (preferably after a point has been completed). You examine it. It is clearly not one of yours. The number of dots is different and they are of a different shape. The manufacturer's name is different from that on the balls you are using. The ball is slightly smaller, livelier, and of a different color—dark green versus yellow. It is clearly not a member of your set.

Conclusion: It must belong to somebody else. But to whom? You can't interrupt play on the adjacent courts to ask, so you must wait till it stops. Action on the court to the right stops first.

"Hey! Are you missing a ball?"

"Yeah." (The traditional response. To say no would be like refusing a drink.)

"Is it green with twelve little shields on it and made by the Wright Brothers?"

There is a conference, followed by a query. "Is there a round, homemade purple dot on it and the initials, K.G.B.?"

You rotate it and peer closely. "G or D?"

"G."

"No. Anyway, your purple is not my purple. I would call the dot more of an off-puce."

"Not ours, then." They resume play, if it can be called that.

Your opponent, meanwhile, is at the net, leaning on the tape to stretch it, because, whenever you start up again, it is his serve.

"For God's sake, Joe. Kick the ball downcourt. The owner will find it eventually. Not too many guys have the same three initials and the same purple dot on their balls. Let's finish up the damn set."

"Hold it," you tell him gently, but firmly. "Got to show some courtesy." A further inquiry elicits the information that it belongs to the proprietors of the court to the left of the other adjacent court. As your opponent fumes, you march down there with the ball, being careful all the while not to get struck by the waving rackets of wild-eyed players.

Finally you get the attention of the presumptive owners.

"This ball rolled onto our court. We're over there." You point to the half-empty court, on which your opponent is swinging his racket hysterically, as though trying to swat a slow-moving wasp.

A cute-looking miss, tanned as far as the eye can see, approaches you, panting prettily.

"Oh, thanks. . . . So sorry to have troubled you. I hope it didn't break up your volley."

"Not a bit. How are you doing, anyway?"

"Joe!!!!" (From your frenetic opponent.)

"Well, I think they're ahead." A determined look. Those legs! "But we'll catch up."

"I hope you do. . . . Don't worry about hitting balls on other people's courts. That's what they're there for." A charming smile and wave—and off to reality.

(Contrast this, *en passant,* with those occasions when *you* are winning, time is about to run out, and a stray ball invades your court. If it came from the left, you run forward, turn, and give a pololike swipe that sends it soaring like a seagull six courts down to the right. "Goddam bastids. Can't keep their own goddam ball on their own goddam court. Ought to be strung up by the heels and shot. Jesus!'' If it came from the right, you pick it up and hit a long fly ball to the farthest left diagonal corner. You flash a look of consummate hatred at all those on your right, including the completely blameless, and take three fiery breaths. Then you resume play—if your opponent is not at the water fountain.)

Then there are the preplanned interruptions. If you are some kind of doctor you can carry around with you a little buzzerlike thing (I don't know what they call them), having left instructions at the hospital for the chief nurse to buzz you every five or ten minutes. It is in your pocket, so nobody can hear it but you. When you're winning, no notice is taken. But when you're falling behind, and it appears that you may easily lose the match within the time allotted, you remember your Hippocratic oath. In the middle of a rally that will probably make the score 5–3, 40–15, his favor, you stop short, produce the buzzer thing, and listen to it. You approach the net.

"Jesus Christ, Murray. I'm sorry, but I got to call in. You can hear the buzzer going.''

Glumly, he concedes he hears something. "For God's sake, you can't play one more point?''

You look shocked. "Hell, no! Somebody could have a busted appendix or something.''

His eyes narrow. "I thought you were the medical administrator there. What the hell could you do for a busted appendix?''

"Nothing, *medically*. But there's a lot of paperwork and if the nurse on duty is kind of dense, the poor guy could die right in the lobby. I got to help her out, shuffle the papers, maybe eliminate some of the questions.''

"Do you remove the appendix then?''

"Depends on how busy we are, the time of day, what surgeon is on duty. Anyway, you've got to be a humanitarian and let me reach a phone. Maybe it's just my wife telling me she's going out bowling with the girls. I'll be right back if I can.''

And you never come back.

The businessman, by contrast, must take his chances. He posts a friend, or a relative, or some kid who wants to make fifty cents to call at, say, 3:30 in the afternoon of a Saturday, after a half-hour's play.

If the tycoon is leading when the attendant runs out with the news that there's an urgent phone call for him, he scoffs at the report.

"Urgent! Baloney [or some stronger word]! That's probably Wickens. Anything that happens on a weekend, they think I have to handle it personally. Probably there's rumblings in the market on account of the soybean sauce we sold—or gave away—to China. Tell him I'll call back when I've finished the match.''

"Sounds like a little kid.''

"That's Wickens's secretary. She *does* sound like a little kid. You've got a good ear for voices, Carl. But let me worry about it. I believe I was serving, with the score thirty-love. . . . These damn interruptions!''

On the other hand, if you happen to be losing and you receive notification of a phone call, an alarm bell goes off. "Holy hell, for me? Jesus, Harry, I was afraid of this. You know that merger we planned with Gifford & Cousins? Well, it's too complicated to go into—but I bet that's news that it fell through. We're going to have to retrench, fast. Listen, I'm awfully sorry about this—it looked like it was going to be one helluva match. I was just getting my forehand going. [A few confident swings.] I'd better take off.''

"But the attendant said it was your wife,'' your opponent protests.

"Yeah, she'd be relaying the message.''

"About picking up some lettuce on the way home.''

"Yeah. . . . It's a kind of code we use. You know this industrial spy situation. I'd better get right to the phone.''

"You can't play one more lousy point?" A grim challenge.
"Jesus, I think I see the next bunch of players filing down
the courts. We wouldn't have time to finish anyway. . . . I'd
better call her back. This could be serious."
And you trot off down the battery of courts, never to be
seen again.

The crossover on odd-numbered games is an excellent
chance to work stalls, because then a kind of pause in one's
labors is reasonably legitimate. (In casual matches, that is.
In tournament tennis, you are allowed one minute to rest, put
on new makeup, towel off, change your shirt, pop in a few
salt pills, find out the score, and see if there is any royalty in
the stands. Should one of the contestants be close to complete collapse, a lenient umpire will allow ten seconds more
unless he gets such a fierce look from the other contestant
that he would rather have a corpse on his hands than face her
wrath.)
In nontournament tennis, the stalling expert—eager to
drive his opponent nuts, run out the clock, or regain what is
left of his health—has numerous ploys at his disposal—and
no umpire to tell him to get his ass on the road. If one's
opponent acts jittery, what better recourse has he than an
implacable stall? I have met players who have an absolute,
inviolable compulsion about never being the first on the
court after the crossover. They are like those people who
never take the far side of the court at the start of a match.
The crossover stallers will towel off four times, from their
shoes to their neck down to their wristwatch and then attack
the racket, the Gatorade bottle, and the bench where they
have been sitting. They adjust their arm and leg supports and
casually change sweaters—from light to heavy and back
again. They root through their equipment bags to try on
visors, Australian hats, headbands, fezzes—whatever the sun
seems to demand at that particular time of day and point of
the solstice.

They put suntan lotion on their noses and sometimes little cardboard things that make them look like characters dancing on the streets of New Orleans during Mardi Gras time. They bang the frame of one racket against the strings of another.

"Which sounds higher to you?" they ask, knowing you are going to lie in your teeth.

Finally, you are so weary of sitting on the bench, cooling off to the point of paralysis, watching your schnook opponent go through his ritual ablutions and listening to his esoteric blather that, to escape, you stride onto the court.

He watches you head there, realizing you are seething. How long can he make you seethe before you either charge off the court, get in your car, drive to a bar, and get smashed—or march over to where he is basking and let him have one across the chops with your racket? It is a fine point. I have come very close to doing both, but was outwitted both times.

Well, he has had his triumph. He has gotten his opponent to venture out onto the court first. Now, like the great John L. Sullivan, he is ready to step into the ring. Everything is tucked away neatly, the bottle cap of the suntan lotion is tightly screwed on, the unused supports are precisely folded and set in their proper place, the powder can is checked to see that there is some left in case an emergency should arise, the hats are returned after the germs have been blown off them, the sweaters have been folded and jammed in. No. Something doesn't quite fit. A pause. Then out everything comes. . . . His backside presents one helluva target. But tennis is, above all else, a game of courtesy.

And the artistic business of making the unwilling opponent stand on the court waiting with egg on his face—to the intense gratification of this particular species of psych artist—goes on at least three times a set, six times a match, and generally many times more.

Is it any wonder that the fourth biggest cause of homicide in America is the tennis staller?

That is not necessarily to say that all stalling is bad. Sometimes it is necessary for survival. But it is one thing to do it blatantly, with an inner wolfish grin, and another to do it subtly—so subtly that your opponents and partner, while in a state of general bewilderment, do not know that delaying tactics are taking place.

What follows is an example of the *subtle* stall.

9

The *Subtle* Stall

Time is relative. An hour can seem like a year, two hours like a decade.

Suppose you are in this position: Invited to play indoor tennis with three so-called friends while enjoying the most raging and trip-hammering of hangovers. You keep looking at the clock on the wall between shots, wondering why the hands never move. An opponent notes your preoccupation.

"How come you keep staring at the clock, Charlie? You got a heavy date or something?" (Ribald snickers from both opponents.)

"Oh, was I watching the clock?" you say innocently. "I just wanted to see if we could finish the set."

"I guess we can. We've got an hour and a quarter left and it's 4-1 in our favor."

My God! you think. They have the damn court for *two hours!* Your stomach churns a little bit. Why in hell did you have those last four highballs? You have simply got to find some desperate ways to stall.

There is always the business, indoors, of arguing about whether the opponents' ball hit the purlins, rafters, and beams overhead. You try it:

"Didn't your shot hit something, Henry?"

"My God, Charlie! That was a drive! I know it cleared the net by about eight feet—but it sure as hell didn't hit any rafters. Ask Gene. Ask your own partner."

Regretfully, Gene has to confirm the opponent's contention. And there is little so ignominious as finding your partner in complete agreement on a technical point with the enemy's side.

So much for that gambit. How many times can shoelaces break in a match? Already twice, while three players, with huge amounts of money invested in all-too-brief indoor court rental, are fuming and fretting and mentally ticking off the seconds as they stand around unable to hit a ball on this expensive piece of real estate. But if a shoelace can break twice, that means it is a rotten shoelace, doesn't it? It could break a third time. Ah, the hell with it. They would get suspicious.

That head! Pound, pound, pound. It feels like a band of malicious elves inside, dancing with clogs on—and applauded by shrieking banshees, all off-key.

The ball goes back and forth. Somebody wins, somebody loses. When you miss, your partner gives you a glare: You are a nonpaying guest. When he misses, you commiserate: He is part-owner of the court. Bad bounce; the light is tricky there; I gave him a setup; you tried to put too much on the ball; you hit it too fine. (Jerk!)

Ha! Examine the ball to see if it has too little air in it. Squeeze, bounce. "I think one of these balls doesn't have enough air in it." Your partner, the last player to have missed a shot, gives you a kind of dubious support. The balls are collected, squeezed, bounced on the clay, compared, and pronounced fit.

"Maybe there's a blind spot on Gene's side of the court," you offer, to explain why Gene missed the shot, then sneak a quick look at the clock on the wall.

"Hey! Wake up! Your serve," says Gene, tossing you two balls.

"I'd like a third. I like to serve with three balls. In case I serve a let and also to make sure that nobody trips over a loose one."

"Since when?" Gene demands. "I've seen you laugh like hell when Julie stepped on one at Memorial, lost his balance, staggered onto the next court, and fell flat on his face. 'Funniest thing I ever saw,' I recall you saying at the time. After you could talk."

"I've reformed," you announce primly.

The third ball is rounded up and carefully placed an inch from the net behind you, rolls a quarter inch and is replaced. Seconds whizzing by. Now to the serve.

Certainly, if one hits the first ball out, that will eat up the clock. Should there be an argument about it by your partner at the net, that will take time. But no faults *into* the net.

Bounce, bounce, bounce. How many bounces can you get away with before serving? Indoors, not too many. The receiver will become apoplectic.

Four bounces. First ball out. Second ball floating (the trajectory will eat up a fraction of a second). Happens three times.

"Jesus Christ!" Gene says, coming back to the baseline to bounce you a ball. "Can't you get the first serve in? Or at least put something on the second one? It's murder up there at the net." His face is a ghastly white.

"Roger," you nod and he goes back to the front. But in this otherworldly condition, you don't have your usual timing and coordination. You hit the first serve on the edge of the frame and it goes sideways—a perfect shank. Gene turns around and gives you a disconsolate look. He turns again, moves back two steps, crouches and places his racket in front of his face, gripping it tight with both hands. But his trepidation is uncalled-for. You double fault.

Well, you are eating up the clock, though serving is robbing you of energy. If you could only get the other three to argue, while you take a quiet, standing-up snooze in backcourt.

Ask and it shall be given.

You serve. There is a short rally. Finally Gene, at the net, puts the ball away.

"I hate to fink on my own partner, but I think Gene leaned over the net." Such a look of awe and outrage from Gene!

"In the first place, I didn't—how could you see from back there?—and in the second it's perfectly legal."

A storm breaks. "Like hell it's legal!" From Henry, striding up to the net. "You can't lean over the net. Maybe you can poke your racket past it, but you can't lean over it!"

"Wait a minute!" Tim joins the battle, waving his racket to emphasize every other syllable he speaks. People back away in alarm when Tim talks to them up close, brandishing a racket—he could break your nose while stressing a point. "You can't put your racket over the net *at any time at all!* That's the rule."

A surreptitious look at the clock. Ah! Seconds flying past like a stream of bats. Inhale deeply to get some of the lost oxygen back.

"Suppose the ball bounces on this side and then bounces back on that side. You mean to tell me you can't reach over for it?"

"That's tough kazovs, baby."

"The rule is, you can reach over the net as long as you don't touch it."

"No! Suppose you touch it *after* you hit the ball? I know that's a legal shot."

"You are *never* allowed to touch the net."

"How about when you string it up? Or measure it?"

"Har-de-har-har."

"Charlie." They turn toward me. "You know the rules. What's the rule?"

The respite is over.

With a sigh: "You're not allowed to reach over the net with your racket until after you've hit the ball on your side of the net. You can follow-through over the net."

"That's crazy." This comment from all three.

"Anyway . . . Jesus Christ! Here we are wasting time arguing and we should be playing! My God, we must have lost three minutes!"

(Five, actually, but who's counting?)

"Anyway, I didn't lean over the net," from an aggrieved Gene.

The score is discussed, the combatants resume their positions and play resumes.

You have become stiff after standing about so long, while the others have been actively arguing, and double-fault the game away. Well, at least the twin responsibilities of getting the ball in that little box and keeping your partner from getting murdered at the net are over.

Now you have a small altercation with Gene as to who should receive where. The opponents give contradictory advice. Purposely, you receive on the wrong side.

"My God!" you say, slapping your forehead (the gesture hurts), after the opponents have won the first two points. "I'm supposed to be receiving in the deuce court!"

"You *are* in the deuce court," Gene says, then explains testily: "The deuce court refers to the position a player assumes on the court when the next point will make it deuce."

"Not if I *win* it," you say dryly.

"He is in the wrong court," Tim announces. "I know because I always worry about him sending a forehand down my alley. He should be over there." He points to the first court, the right court, the deuce court, the forehand court. "Besides, the deuce court is the right-hand court. The advantage court is always the left, or backhand, court."

You start walking over there.

"Hey, wait a minute!" Tim yells. "You can't change courts in the middle of game!"

"Yes, we can," insists Gene, a logician. "And the game starts over."

There are anguished howls from the opponents, who are in nearly complete agreement. They move forward aggressively.

"As a matter of fact," asserts Tim, "you should forfeit the game, because that could be considered cheating."

"I don't know about that," says Henry, "but suppose they keep changing sides all through the game. All we are facing is forehands. That's like Mickey Mantle batting for Phil Rizzuto and Roger Maris batting for Tommy Henrich, then Mantle batting for Yogi Berra and Maris batting for Joe Gordon. That is some lineup.''

"How the hell could Mantle bat for Berra? He'd be on base.''

"Put in a runner for him.''

"Who you got? Who would you put in?''

"Hell, I don't know. Casey Stengel.''

"From the Mets?''

"Hell, Casey is retired and Yogi is no longer manager of the Mets; besides, all those other guys you're talking about are retired.''

"So what? It's a helluva concept.''

"Hey, fellas,'' Gene interrupts. "All this baseball palaver is fascinating, but we're running out of time. I don't think I've hit a ball in the past twenty-five minutes.''

"Small loss,'' Henry remarks flippantly.

"Well, let's get back to the game. Start it over.''

"Start over, hell! It's thirty–love.''

Tim pulls up short on his way back to the baseline. "Hey! I just thought of something. If they switch sides in the middle of a game, that means you're serving to Earl twice in a row.''

(God knows you are falling apart, though there are not many more hills to climb.)

"Suppose Gene and I change sides again,'' you offer.

"But that puts you on the wrong side,'' Henry objects. "And then I suppose it's thirty-love, *your* favor.''

"Suppose we play on the same side,'' you offer with an éclat you are far from feeling

"You *are* on the same side—oh, I see what you mean.''

Gene wails, "Let's get on with this thing. We've got three minutes left. I even forgot what the score was.''

"You would,'' says Henry. "It's 5-1.''

"Can't be,'' you point out calmly. "It's got to be an odd number. Henry served first.''

"Call it anything you like!'' wails Gene. "Serve the goddam ball!''

Already the vultures who have the next hour or two hours

on the court are assembling on the sidelines, one eye on the clock, one eye on the incompetent clowns gamboling in their last throes—probably digging the court up, too.

The ball is served.

"Time!" yells one of the newcomers as Gene is about to swing.

Gene utters a terrible word and whacks the ball as hard as he can. It sails up and up and hits one of the overhead lights, extinguishing it and plunging one entire corner of the court into darkness.

There is some sort of consternation on the sidelines.

"Bravo," says Henry to Gene in a low voice as everyone moves off the court.

The guard changes, accompanied by a discussion among the newcomers as to who will play nighttime tennis in the Stygian corner.

"One of you birds tell George at the desk the light is busted," orders a newcomer.

All four of you start to giggle! Quelle timing!

"Sure," Gene assures him, his hand slyly covering his mouth. "We'll tell him." He buckles over.

He is called something under the newcomer's breath that he affects not to hear. At another time, in another place, it would have meant a punch in the eye. But tennis, if nothing else, is a game of courtesy. The deadly, provocative insult is ignored. Maybe Gene will meet him on the Field of Honor someday.

On the way out, burdened with coats, equipment, and various other baggages, Tim says, "Hey! I got an idea! Let's finish this up on the asphalt courts at Allenwood!"

"I got a better one," says Henry. "Let's all go to the Village Inn and get loaded!"

A brilliant thought. To relax these tired old muscles.

"Second it."

You march out, four warriors after battle.

Hair of the dog.

10

Knotty Problems

Because, as a student of the technical aspects of tennis, I probably know more about the rules than anyone in the United States—not necessarily just for the purpose of taking advantage of them—I am often sent letters by tennis players and curious spectators who know my reputation as a fair arbiter of squabbles on and off the court and an untangler of knotty problems.

I receive about a thousand letters a month, most of which are not of great significance to the tennis world and which I burn. But there are some queries I get in the mail that have a kind of general and universal import for serious tennis players when they are answered with expert, considered judgment.

Here are some of them:

Q.   In dashing up to the net after a first serve in doubles, where should one hit the opening volley? *(T.R.C., Newark, N.J.)*

A.   On the racket strings, if possible; or on the racket throat—risky but an almost sure winner if the ball lands in the opponents' court.

Q.   Towards the end of a close match, with both players furious at one another and involved in a duel at the net, Player A, that lovable rogue, swatted a ball at B's midsection, knocking him flat onto his back and cutting down on his night life, if you know what I mean. B, gasping and moaning, claimed the match because of A's impulsive action. Is he justified? *(M.D., Little Neck, N.Y.)*

A.   These things happen. The ruling is, if B could not continue, he should default. If he *can* continue, A should default.

Q.   Do you think P. J. Sutton, the great English stylist, could beat any of the World's First Ten? *(R.K.V., Betternot, Miss.)*

A.   Frankly, no—but you have to remember he is now ninety-four years old.

Q.   In a tournament semifinal, Player A was so upset by a linesman's call and his own botches that, when the score reached 2-0, he became sulky and sat all squinched up beneath the umpire's chair, muttering to himself. His opponent began swearing and making the "Balkan peace sign" to the spectators when he found no one to serve to. Finally he broke his racket over the foot-fault judge's head. What is your opinion as to the disposition of the players? *(G. McV., Troy, N.Y.)*

A.   Pretty miserable.

Q.   If I see the ball good and my opponent does not, what should I do? *(O.P.R., Niles, Ohio)*

A.   You should beat his tail off.

Q.   What happens in a senior doubles final of a local tournament if the umpire and the linesmen fail to show up? *(R.G.T., Madrid, Ga.)*

A.   You get some funny calls.

Q.   Where does a tennis ball travel faster—at the Equator or the North Pole? *(M.S.G., Durant, Tex.)*

A. Depends on who hits it.

Q. As you know, in some tournament singles matches, singles sticks are placed near the ends of the net to raise it 1.28 inches. Because the tournament committee was in a hurry to get to a hoedown before the doubles final of a tournament in which I was participating, this match was played without the singles sticks being removed—making the net 1.28 inches higher at the ends than it should have been.

As a result, some of my shots hit the net tape, instead of sailing in for sure points if the net had not been raised at the ends. Do I (1) have any recourse in that the match should be replayed with the singles sticks removed? and (2) should the opponents forfeit because they realize my shots would have gone over the net for sure points under different circumstances? *(R.V.R. RFD #3, Patchogue, N.Y.)*

A. Yes to both questions, if it can be demonstrated that the net was higher on your side than it was on your opponents'.

Q. What do Don Budge and Rod Laver have in common? *(G.G.G., Pompano Beach, Fla.)*

A. The number of letters in both their first and last names. Bil Baird, the puppeteer, is also in this select group.

Q. What is a tie-buster? *(H.P. Jr., Creedmore Hospital, N.Y.)*

A. Something you wear around your neck, buddy.

Q. In an important doubles match, Jones hit a smash from midcourt, but his racket slipped from his hand and slithered under the net into the opponents' court. While the rally continued, Jones, to retrieve his racket, crawled under the net and became entangled in it, unable to extract himself. Eventually he reached his racket but, as his partner hollered,

"Let! Let!" he was half-strangled by the cord that holds up the net. What would your decision be? (*J.G.R., Montgomery, Ala.*)

A.   That somebody had better get Jones out of there before he chokes to death.

Q.   In the illustrious hundred-year history of tennis, with all the classic innovative methods of striking the ball exemplified by the great players—such as Johnston's topspin forehand; H. H. Jacobs's chop; Vines's flat backhand; Rosewall's slice backhand; Kramer's slice serve; Hoad's smash; B. J. King's forehand volley; Segura's two-handed forehand; Fraser's twist serve, Larsen's drop shot; and Laver's topspin lob—altogether how many kinds of shots are there? *(C.G.H.F., London, England)*

A.   Two. Good and bad.

Q.   In the final of an important national tournament in one of the less-developed but economically wealthy Eastern countries, a rope was used instead of a net and a special net judge was seated on a carpet beneath it to determine if the balls during play crossed over or under it.

This official apparently did not understand the main objectives of tennis, because he applauded enthusiastically every time a ball flew under the rope, and then went to sleep. (It was 140° in the shade and the only shade in this treeless land is furnished by oil derricks.) The height of the net kept changing, since it was the Day of the Feast of T'qrut-T'rqat and the rope at the time was being used for a tug-of-war between two crack camel regiments, about 800 on a side.

When the score reached 6–all, my opponent, the local champion, refused to serve unless the rooters for each team calmed down and stopped chewing betel nuts. (Incidentally, the local emir is not too crazy about foreigners, of which I am one.) Because some of the camels got loose and were being chased around the court by shouting spectators, the playing surface, which was made of natural products, started to get badly ripped up.

Since I realized that bounces during rallies would be erratic, I resolved to dash to the net. When my opponent finally served, I hit a deep ball down the middle and sprinted forward, almost immediately sinking to my hips. The umpire, the local pasha, not only did not call a let (it is one of the four words in the language I understand) but insisted that play continue on subsequent points while I struggled to clamber out of the pit I was in and while hysterical camels and janissaries were invading my court. Do you think I should continue playing the set? (*A.L.G., formerly of Garden City. N.Y.*)

A. It is better than Sudden Death.

Q. When is it advisable for a player to choke his racket? (*T. O'T., Louisville, Kans.*)

A. Whenever he loses his temper because the racket is not hitting the ball where he aims it.

Q. We play very tough tennis out here in Indiana, and in a mixed doubles match the male opponent kept swatting balls at my partner at the net. The first few times he did it I politely warned him, and the next time he did it, instead of retaliating by directing shots at his partner's behind, at the crossover I hauled off and popped him with a straight right, knocking him cold, and then poured iced tea over his three extra rackets. The umpire (female) chewed me out for my impulsive behavior, but I think I was justified. Is chivalry dead? (*[Mrs.]G.R.V., Gary, Ind.*)

A. And buried.

Q. Because of the crowded court situation in my home town, several friends of mine and I get on a court with four on a side and whale away with two rackets each—one in each hand. There have been several broken rackets and a few minor concussions but nothing serious. (We are all using metal rackets now.) Do you have any suggestion for making the contest more interesting? (*M.A.S.H., Hollywood, Calif.*)

A. Yes. Introduce a ball into the game.

11

Confrontation
with a Lady Tennis Champ

Before becoming a hustler, as I should not have to point out, I was a prominent internationalist with a large number of tough wins under my belt. Here is the background, hitherto unrevealed, of the most dramatic of them all.

Billy Forester and I were in the men's locker room at the West Side Tennis Club in Forest Hills, New York, cutting up old touches and exchanging philosophies, just before my match with Zammer of Germany, the European champion. He was standing indolently by a locker and I was seated with my feet up to get the blood flowing uphill. Forester had won some kind of consolation final against that soccer player from Rumania and was feeling pretty expansive. He had his bottle out and every once in a while, when I gave him a strong look, he would refill my Dixie cup. It was horrible stuff.

"Let me throw this at you, Forester," I said, listening occasionally to faint crowd roars from the stadium, which was about two furlongs away. "Have you any brains? Are you listening? Let us say this cutie—she has a good forehand, an okay backhand, can run like hell, and has the knack of long-distance seduction so that the linesmen tend to give her the benefit of the close ones (forcing her opponent to do some lavish winking and murmuring and hip-waggling herself)—so then, suddenly, by the luck of the draw, she is your mixed doubles partner.

"Now you know and I know—from your wild experiences in Petoskey, Michigan, and Tonawanda, New York—"

"North Tonawanda."

"—that before you step on the court with her, she is either going to slip into the sack with you or she ain't."

"That is a safe premise," he conceded, pouring another shot for me and arranging for an even bigger belt for himself.

"Where do you scrape up your liquor, Forester? Because this is stultifying stuff." I forced the concoction down for medicinal and psychological reasons. Zammer, it was reported, had not lost a set—or was it point?—in three years. Word had reached me that if you tried to return his forehand from in front of the baseline, your arm immediately became numb and you could not lift a glass for two months. Terrifying thought. But, thank God, somebody—Liggett & Myers maybe?—had invented straws. Also, fortunately, I am kind of ambidextrous in that area.

"Damn, I'm nervous about this cat, Forester," I said, extending my cup, which he refilled, looking heavenward but never spilling a drop. "Have you seen him play?"

"Yeah. In Berne. Roller-skating, skiing, the whole bit. All-around athlete. He'll run you into the ground. Never misses and every shot is a killer. If you hit a ball that lands more than an inch from the baseline, he's down your throat. Hasn't missed a volley in four years."

I took a big swallow, musing and projecting. The fellow must have *some* weakness. "Is he any kind of a psych artist? Because I am not too bad in that area myself. I took out a couple of linespersons night before last and told them the kind of calls I expect. Good calls. My battle plan is to hit deep—a little beyond the line, maybe into a linesperson's lap—and if he thinks the calls are questionable he might throw all his rackets into the stands, or over them, and have to retire. . . . Pour me one. . . . You know what's odd? Here are Zammer and I, playing for about fifty thousand smackers in prize money and I must have laid out about the same amount in wining and dining two linespeople."

"Well, you've always got endorsements," he said, then smiled enigmatically. "I bet if you laid out twenty-three dollars your guests would have died from shock. Come now, you took out the baseline lineslády and tried to get her stewed on ten dollars, and now you're worried that if you hit a ball beyond the rear service line she's going to call it out."

"You named it, Forester," I admitted. "Linespersons can destroy you. And speaking of destruction—one for the highway please—I know this Teuton is going to come up to the net on me. Unnatural. Where are the days of white flannels and cries of 'Peach!' and baseline rallies where you could lose a point with dignity? Slam, bam, thank you, ma'am. That is neo-modern tennis. When was the last time a server lost his serve? I'd guess 1971." To calm my frayed nerves, I took a giant swallow and then grimaced as if I'd learned that I had a sudden appointment with the IRS and my wife's barrister on the same afternoon. "How can you drink this horrible stuff?"

To prove he could, he took an even bigger slug. Cough, hack, drool, rolling of the eyes, throaty noises, then the whole performance was repeated like a rerun.

"You're putting me on, Forester. Nobody could make all those noises and survive." He handed me the bottle like it was a live hand grenade he had to get rid of. Half empty. I took a swig before he had a change of heart. "Phew! Waugh! Wodehouse! What bad stuff!" I exclaimed, when my larynx would listen to reason. "Forester, I figure you have a bet on this European usurper and are trying to poison me so I won't have the strength to scream at the umpire."

He gave me a bland look, which could be interpreted in many ways. Poison? No. He winced in anticipation of what he was doing to his viscera and forced down another swallow. It was a cozy scene: Me about to go out and fight for the Open Championship against a hitter tennis experts claimed could tear your arm off with a forehand. Forester, my old buddy, whom I had played against and partnered in doubles (I had to push him around the court and remind him if he didn't get the second serve in we would lose the point); but we were still doubles champs of Malta, the Far East, and the nightclub circuit. And here he was, trying to get me loaded so I would lose the first point, the first game, and the first set and then have to overcome insuperable odds.

While I was reflecting with a certain amount of bitterness, assembling grievances, and getting my cup refilled (for increased clarity of thought), Sophie came in—followed by autograph hounds, reporters, fans, TV people with their roving cameras, and lighting experts, and preceded by her bosom, which was startling.

It seemed she had just won the Ladies' Open and was aglow with triumph. Dark hair, round blue eyes, tanned wherever you could see (which was nearly everywhere), beautiful teeth, for which you probably would never have to pay a dentist to get them fixed or filled, the sturdiest legs in the Northern Hemisphere and a cute button nose (if you ever worked up that high). You could even see the muscular striations in her belly, if you looked close enough, which I was too polite to do.

"Jesus Jumping Christ, Sophie," I said, as Forester imperiously shooed her entourage back out of the door. I gave her the light tennis player's handshake, she being right-handed. "I guess you are to be congratulated, winning your first Nationals, considering what some people might call a handicap, but which would make a sculptor, if you posed nude for him, dance with delight."

She made such a subtle nod of acknowledgment that I hesitate to describe it. It said, "Whatever you will of me, Grand master, I will do it."

You talk about your great historic confrontations—Omar Khayyam and King Solomon, Samson and Gomorrah, Tennyson and Guinevere, "The Hammer" and the Kansas City offensive line, me and Don on the iceberg, me and

Hughes when we both had the idea of garageing our own
atom bomb and met face mask to face mask twenty-four
fathoms down. Ali's nape of the neck and Wepner's round-
house right, David and Saul, David and Mrs. Simpson, and
many others, for history is an on-going phenomenon—this
outranked all of them.

Here we two were in our first fleshly confrontation.
Naturally, she had seen me before, in photos, on the screen,
on a dozen talk shows; as I had seen her in the same media,
though at a ratio, I presumed, of forty to one.

I should mention that she was wearing a very snazzy tennis
dress made by Tingaling, the famous English tennis-dress
designer, consisting of washable polyester cotton, gently
shaped at the waist, with ravishing double-stripe trim in
bright navy blue and a V-neck down to her navel, ribbed
cuffs, action-cut sleeves and the Czechoslovak eagle emblazoned over the left-side pocket. Altogether smashing—the
fact of which, it can be projected, she was not unaware. They
probably sold a million of them the following morning.
Sometimes when she talked, her tummy kind of rotated, but
that might have been my imagination, plus the congreves in
Forester's liquor.

I made a circular motion with my finger, palm down, and
she prettily complied. It reminded you of a fashion show and
a slave auction but was somehow different from either. As I
suspected, she had the most beautiful bottom in the world,
and it was uncovered to the extent of good taste, thanks to
the multifold genius of Tingaling. I had a sudden on-the-spot
fantasy of serving when she was my partner at net. Com-
munication by tennis ball. Whacko! And she would rub the
spot gently and move over to her left to cover more of the
alley.

"I can't cover your alley and race to my right to retrieve a
wide crosscourt at one and the same time." That is what the
ball would be saying to her. Schizophrenic I ain't—not yet,
anyway.

"Hey, Forester, we're pretty dry down here. The both of us are." A smile of flamboyant gratitude. He produced another Dixie cup for the lady champion and reluctantly poured a couple of belts.

She was sort of quietly raping me with her matching big blue eyes. When, I wondered idly, would we touch? Because that would be an explosion of considerable note. Rockets going off. Volcanoes. Planets colliding. Armageddon. The Apocalypse. All in one bag.

"Look here, Sophie," I said, "if I may call you by your first name on this short acquaintance—you just beat this Libber with the buck teeth and glasses, the one that gave Bobby such a hard time—"

"King."

"Yeah. Used to call herself Moffett. Good volley but she don't understand spin. Hey!—" sudden thought—"that makes you champion of the world, doesn't it? (Ladies' version.)"

"I didn't win Wimbledon yet."

"Where were you at Wimbledon? I won all three, with Forester here and some Alsatian cutie that I used to keep telling what the score was in French-German and posting her between points in the right spot. Come to think of it, Zammer was on the other side, with some cutie from Ceylon with great teeth. No dental bills there. . . . I think she married the service linesman later. At least she owed him that, after some of the calls she was getting.

"There was one serve I made, to the deuce court. The ball was at least two inches in and this crazy old man, being it was game point, suddenly woke up for a split second and made an 'out' gesture. You can imagine my reaction, even though I had one serve left.

"I ran over and started swatting things—the legs of his chair, then the net tape, reducing it to shreds, then the umpire's feet, making him curl them up like a fugitive raccoon in a tree trying to escape from a pack of baying

Making the umpire curl
up like a fugitive raccoon in a tree

bloodhounds and all the while screaming—more for effect than from true emotional upset—'When Mr. G. hits a slice serve to the right-hand corner of the deuce court, it always goes in! Unless he purposely knocks it out—like a sportsmanship gesture on those infrequent occasions when you fools make a bad call against one of his opponents!''

"The crowd was hurling pillows and beer cans and shoes onto the court—whatever they could lay hands on. Fights were going on in the stands, like at an international soccer match. The umpire kept pleading over the PA system for some kind of order. Fans began scaling pillows at their least-favorite linesman. I began reading the rulebook, but Zammer, with a wolfish grin, was scaling them back into the stands—not haphazardly, but *aiming* them. I don't know if I told you, but he was (and is) one of the great sidearm leg bowlers in cricket.

"Gulp. Whew!" Punction by Sophie, eyes awater.

"Hey, Forester," I said. "The little lady's cup seems to be empty. Suppose you refill it."

He held the bottle upside down, then looked through it like a spyglass, the neck held to his eye. Then, with a sigh you could hear in Keokuk, Iowa, he opened the locker and produced a second, or third, or whatever it was.

"Grand master," said Sophie, "that was a fascinating tale about Zammer. Here's luck in your match."

She downed everything in her cup, then had a slight, but sophisticated, coughing fit, as if she wanted to continue but couldn't find the proper tubes for it, the liquor attacked by gravity and her breath was being expelled in another direction.

I gave her a sharp, therapeutic smack on the back. As I expected, rockets went off. Her eyes expanded like two blue balloons and she staggered around the locker room, banging lockers, knocking over restrung tennis rackets, and spilling the pro's bucket of tennis balls, clutching Forester for support, then me (longer), releasing a bunch of pigeons prematurely—that were to signal the beginning of the match between Zammer and myself—and in general wreaking havoc.

Finally she got control of herself and sat down. Remember, she had just played a tough three-setter with the young lady who thought she could beat Riggs.

"Let me throw something at you," said Forester, "you talking about bad calls. My feeling is you don't need linesmen and all that paraphernalia."

"Opponent makes the calls," I suggested dreamily.

"No, you fool! He'll cheat the ass off you—unless he is setting you up for something. You make your own calls! When I hit a shot—say a lob—I've had enough experience to know the moment I hit it whether it is going in or out. . . . I don't have to tell *you,* Mr. G."

I toasted his acknowledgment of my powers.

"I know it is going in, so what do I need a linesman for? If I hit it long purposely, I know it is going long and I don't need him or her to inflate his or her ego by screaming 'Out!' "

I nodded. A good point. "Maybe you could make the decision and, like a third-base umpire, pass it along to the chief linesman who would pass it along to the linesman most concerned. Then he would know what to call and act accordingly. Then you have the real drama of somebody hollering 'Out!', you would inflate your own peculiar ego, Forester—and pour me one more before I go out and murder that bum."

He slopped one in the general direction of my cup. We were out of phase for awhile but then, by reversing my field, I caught up with him and wound up with a man-size drink.

"Sophie," I said, giving her a little whack on the thigh to return her to the real world, "I am not much one for planning ahead, but let us assume that we are playing on the same side in mixed doubles. Against another mixed team. Are you right court or left court or in the middle? Because I am not too crazy about ladies taking over my area of the court."

Sophie kind of readjusted her skirt, if you could call it that. Proud thighs! I was thinking.

"Sophie," Forester said with a kind of evil chuckle, "you are in for an experience if you are on the same side of the net with Mr. G. It is bad enough playing against him, them cuts and all, but when you are on the same side, with him taking every ball—even when you receive serve—you will wind up in the looney bin."

"Hey, Forester," I chided him, "didn't we win Wimbledon the first time they paired us up? I can't be too bad. Taking a green kid (so pour, you dumb bastard. Give my friend here a shot, too) that I had to tell him the distinction between a ground stroke and a volley and guided him to laurels that he has not seen the equal of since."

In an expansive mood, I decided to give Sophie the benefit of a reminiscence and Forester a brief journey into nostalgia.

"So who are we up against in the final? Bunny Austin and von Cramm. On their turf, by which I mean grass. I am a cement player myself, a little bit of carpet if it is carefully swept—"

"Don't forget India."

"—listing cruisers, canvas on ice, ice, etc., etc. But grass? I don't know. There is, of course, all kinds of grass. Poa, Kentucky blue, Bermuda, sharp-bladed, crab, fescue, rye, slanting, crew cut, humble, proud, intransigent, and so forth.

"Well, at Wimbledon they are not going to pour truckloads of cement over grass that maybe Robin Hood gamboled on just for my benefit. So there was nothing for me to do but go to the center court late one night and talk to it. Four in the morning, the place deserted, except for some cats and a groundskeeper or two, and me on my hands and knees cajoling the grass to 'Be nice, be nice.' I guess you know I talk with good effect to tennis balls and my racket cover. Wheedling talk. Some people scoff, but it works for *me*.

"So I am making pretty good headway, dozing off every now and then because it is balmy out, Big Ben tolling off the quarter hours and all. Then suddenly some big cop in blue is standing over me with a lantern, they call them, shining in my eyes. A bobby. A peeler.

"He asked me very respectfully what in hell did I think I was doing, with the queen coming the next day and all. I told him frankly, I was talking to the grass. 'Be nice, be nice.' Petting it, smoothing it. Making promises—more fertilizer, maybe.

"The next thing I knew I was being hoisted up and flung into a patrol waggon, with two Gs, headed toward the constabulary, which is their polite way of saying drunk tank.

"We get there. Arraigned, booked, fingerprinted, mugged; a few small bottles, some funny money I had on me confiscated—they call them pounds over there—and into stir. With the weirdest bunch of cuckoos you ever saw.

"One guy, a Cockney, had half his hair shaved off. Maybe a whim, maybe he had half a brain operation. With a tic, a patch over one eye, right out of Dickens. They took all my pencils away but left this character with a stiletto. He was paring his nails with it. A man/woman next to him, drowsy, in a skirt, berouged, high heels covering the biggest, ugliest feet you ever saw. Huddled in a corner was a Teddy Boy, dressed like Prince Edward, starched cuffs, fur collar, black patent leather shoes you don't lace up. You button them. Cuff links! He must have had to mug about forty old gentlemen to amass the scratch for those cuff links. If you ever saw a doorknob, that is what they looked like."

"I saw a doorknob in 1948," Forester said with a smirk at Sophie. A rival, I concluded.

"Pour and shut up," I said. "Give Sophie one on the house."

"I hate to be a bluenose," Forester intoned, but pouring. "But you are overdue out there." Nor did he neglect his own appetite.

"Who else?" I reflected, aware that Sophie, despite a kind of torpid expression, was hanging on my every word. "Yeah. There was this high-class-looking fella, turned out to be an abortionist. Top hat, tails, on his way to the opera when they nailed him performing his specialty in the back seat of a hansom. What he claimed, anyway. Personally, I think—abortions are legal in Europe—he was merely trying to stab somebody and figured it is better to be locked up as an overzealous abortionist than as a dangerous armed robber. Besides that, the victim wasn't pregnant, and it was a man. 'I would hate to be your solicitor,' I told him after I learned his story.

" 'Back to reality,' I thought. 'About ten hours from now,' I reminded myself, 'I have to be on center court, trying to stand up during four national anthems—' " Puzzled looks. "—Forester's is 'Little Brown Jug.' Bow to royalty, fake a handshake with two opponents, listen to the umpire's instructions: 'Mr. G., if one of our linespeople should make a questionable call—and that has been known to happen—we do not want you hitting Herr Baron Gottfried von Cramm or Mr. Bunny Austin over the elbow with your racket. If you are given the benefit of what you presume is a bad call, we would prefer not to see the statesmanlike gesture of your hitting the next shot over the stadium into the Thames. . . .'

" *'But suppose I am not there!'*

"The specter was a shattering one. I ran to the bars and started shaking them. It worked for Cagney. Finally the sheriff came, or whatever they call them. 'We bailed you out in two world wars,' I shouted at him. 'And here you are, jailing me because you think I am an affluent American. Why the hell aren't you limey bastards out chasing Jack the Ripper and Guy Fawkes, or bus drivers who give you a strange look when you don't furnish the proper change, or kids to whom a sports car muffler is anathema, or guys who bounce a ball fifteen times before serving, or bartenders who don't give you a free one after you have already laid down cash for three?'

"He was wincing. I changed from defense to attack. 'James Mason's teeth are capped. George IV was vastly overweight. Name me twelve English heavyweights who could knock down Rocky Marciano. Where the hell did you get the idea every stone weighed exactly fourteen pounds? You serve warm beer! You spell funny! I am going to hit to Austin's backhand tomorrow—if I ever get the hell out of here!' I shook the bars, using precious energy.

"Finally they let me have thruppence tuppenny, or whatever the coinage is—they never heard of decimals, no wonder we had to bail them out—and I called the U.S. Embassy and a guy came over in striped pants with a letter on vellum from the ambassador in his attache case, and I bade the gaol, as they call it, a fond farewell. 'Sew your own goddam mailbags!' was my parting shot as I slipped into the Rolls and we tooled silently to the people's house where I was staying."

"For reasons of economy," Forester explained gratuitously.

"Forester is kidding you, Soph," I said, reading him. "I am the last of the big spenders."

"If the USLTA wasn't furnishing the balls, you wouldn't see him out there at all," Forester asserted. "But let him tell you about the time he bought a drink for Arnold Palmer. The legend grows with the years."

I looked around, kind of dreamily. "Look here, Forester. I came in here with three rackets. I sure as hell am not going to play this foreigner bare-handed." The screams and shrieks of the crowd were by this time penetrating the locked locker-room door.

"Hey-hey, hoo-ha, Gib, Gib, Gib!"

"Looka here, Sophie doll," I said, a hand friendlylike on

her knee, approximately. "After I crush this usurper, how about you and I doing the picturesque town of Forest Hills together? I know a place where the Martinis are thirty-five cents a throw, but you better carry a razor with you. You got a razor?"

She nodded solemnly. Just at that point Jackie Karter, who was running the tournament, and Gustavus Adolphus IV were spotted by Forester. He apprised me.

"Jesus Kee-rist, Forester," I said in alarm. "They can't find Sophie in the men's locker room!"

"Yes, they can," he asserted. "She's right here."

"I mean they *mustn't*," I said patiently (for me). "They'll take her damn trophy away."

"I go with that," he said. "But where can you hide somebody in a locker room?"

Our eyeballs started working. Both of us got the same idea simultaneously: "In the locker!"

I stood up and fell flat on my face. This is going to be tougher than I thought, I mused. Forester helped me up. "Maybe I should stuff you in the locker and send out Sophie to play Zammer," he muttered.

It was that questionable hootch. It did something to my balance muscles. "Forester," I said, "in every endeavor there has to be a leader and a follower—"

"Spare me the samples," he said and bent down.

"We pick her up and stuff her in the locker on 'three.' "

"Right."

"Three!" I shouted kind of excitedly, for I could hear steps on the steps. We picked Sophie up and staggered over to the locker with her, a distance of about five feet, but I'd guess she was raped (optically) about twelve times.

"Now that we got her here," I panted, "it is up to you to open the locker. I am kind of spent, plus I must face Zammer before the stadium is torn down. I need another belt."

"First things first." He opened the locker and we puffed and heaved and finally got her inside, then forced the door shut. Something was sticking out—a white piece of cloth, orlon acrylic ribbed polyester trimmed in bright navy.

"Can't have that," muttered Forester. He tried to shove it back through. No luck. He gave me a sly wink and placed his forefinger alongside his nose, like an owl.

"Sure as hell there will be an investigation," I commented.

Out she came, wearing a glazed look. Up and over, and suddenly Forester had a tennis costume the size of a guest towel in his hands and I had Sophie in my arms. Splendid preparation for what I knew would be the toughest match of my career.

"Back with her," said Forester.

Reluctantly I helped him maneuver her inside the locker, a pretty and amenable package.

I started to leave, picking up some rackets, possibly mine, and Forester, not a bad skate, stuck a quart bottle into Sophie's arms before closing the door on her. Muffled sounds came from within. Puzzled, I asked Forester what they meant.

"I think she said, 'Was the grass cooperative, Mr. G?' " he replied.

"Two knocks for no, three for yes. Give her three knocks, Forester."

He did so and then staggered to the door to entertain, or hoodwink, his guests. It was me they were after, I was almost sure.

And he suddenly fell down in a stupor, snoring, before reaching the knob.

What can you say about a man who can't hold his liquor?

That was my introduction to Sophie.

12

A Quiet Walkabout

"Gib! Gib! Gib!" came from the stands. Thunderclaps of noise that echoed off all the buildings. I could hear the umpire over the PA, urging the spectators to quiet down—reassuring them that a delegation had been dispatched to "fetch him." (Me.) (A delegation consisting of the second-greatest player America had ever produced, who was also the president and founder of the PTAA and the Grand Panjandrum of American and International tournaments—that would be Jackie. And accompanying him, the regal monarch who had done more to popularize tennis in his native country than anyone in history—ignoring the fact that, in those days, when he became king, lawn tennis had not been invented yet.)

I tried to orient myself. First I took a few deep breaths to get the old eyes to focusing. Then I massaged my wrists to get the blood circulating, meanwhile, jumping up and down to restore some feeling to my feet. I sure hope to God I didn't forget to put my shoes on, I thought. I knew if I looked down I would fall flat on my face.

I began walking—if you could call it that—toward the center of the noise.

"Hey, Arnie!" I called. Arnold Palmer was approaching me, for once without his clubs. "You still owe me for that drink I bought you in Vegas!" Preoccupied with his many businesses, I suppose, he passed right by me and, when I looked back (and got somehow tangled in a hedge), *he* looked back. If he wants to stiff me, that's all right, I rationalized. The poor bastard needs the money to buy a new plane. A dollar ninety-seven down the drain, when money was worth something, back in the fifties.

Two men in blue extracted me from the hedge and gave me a friendly shove in the general direction of the marquee. It was a long way off. In years to come, they will have a moving sidewalk between the bar at the clubhouse and the baseline at center court, I reflected.

That reminded me of Forester. He was probably lapping up the sauce like there was no tomorrow, calling his bookie and placing a few bets on Zammer, then remembering my reputation and hedging and betting a few big ones on me, if he could find any takers.

A turn here, a turn there, the cheers receding. Suddenly I was on the street, cars and buses whizzing by, newshawkers announcing the score—love-all—everything moving three-and-a-half times as fast as it should.

I clutched my rackets, wandering down the treelined street. "Gib, Gib, Gib!" I was still in Forest Hills. Or was that coming from a TV set? How much change have I got? I asked myself. A cozy bar beckoned. Maybe I would see myself on TV. But I would have to be playing—simple logic—and I could not be playing while I was watching myself in a cozy bar.

My capital was five dollars and fifty-six cents, enough for six shots, plus two thrown in if the innkeeper was a sport, plus two beers, to kind of soften the blows of the congreves in alcohol, or whatever you call them.

A quiet entry. It was dark, but no darker than some indoor courts to which I have been invited, nor was the ceiling any lower. Regulars at the bar, I presumed, firm in their convictions, preoccupied with trivia—local gossip, who got a speeding ticket, a report of a fishing expedition.

Some stupid prizefight was on TV, the commentary submerged by a pair of tavern experts arguing over whether more people spoke Chinese than English.

"Depends on what country you're in," I told them, and that shut them up for a while.

I ordered a shot and a beer from the monolith behind the bar, not caring particularly about the brand names, just so I could keep my buzz on until I was face to face with Zammer and could send him back to Baden-Baden in a pine box.

The barkeeper slopped down the drinks, wiped off the mahogany with a rag that must have been used to clean the engines of the old Great Eastern and hovered over me till I fished out some money.

"How many jumps would a four-legged bullfrog need to cross Queens Boulevard?" the cat next to me demanded. I supposed it was a riddle, for there did not seem to be any practical value in knowing the answer.

"Six," I told him. Completely zonked out. Without any acknowledgment, he stumbled over to a booth and was immediately transported to dreamland.

"Turn on the tennis for a minute," I said to the bartender. He gave me a well-here's-somebody-from-Mars look but reached up and did as I requested.

"That's me! That's me!" I shouted, after the squiggles and squaggles had composed themselves into a fairly recognizable picture.

It was me against Sedgman in L.A.—or maybe Reykjavik. Me looking up into the sun—Sedgman was not the clean player they made him out to be; he lobbed into the sun just like Heffernan would—smash, smash, smashing an unreturnable. Called out!

"That ball was in!" I shouted to the quivering set. "I leave it to you" . . . to the stranger, nearly toothless and with lumpy skin, seated to my left.

"Hook him! Hook him!" he was shouting at the screen. Sedgman had been replaced by Nasser in a fast kaleidoscope. "When the hell did I play Nasser?" I asked myself half aloud, and sought insight from the shot glass.

"Whoo! Whoo-ee, woo-ah!" Eyes watering, I had to bang my chest to get my lungs in phase. Combined with Forester's blended rotgut, this was a real potent drink. I drained half the beer to mix the congreves with malt and restore the balance of my metabolism—what was left of it.

Nasser was resigning. Or ripping off masks from various wives and reacting badly. Either that or taking over Aswan. I squinted at the set, separating and converging like an accordion. Imagine yourself trying to return a Mach 4 ball, with topspin yet, I thought. The prospect was terrifying. I better have a couple more shots, I decided. I produced some more money.

"Hey, buddy," came a hoarse voice two chairs down on my right. "How come you're dressed funny like that. In white underwear and painting shoes."

"I'm supposed to be playing for the National Tennis Championship," I told him.

"In here?" He sounded incredulous.

"No. On the TV. Up there." Pointing.

"That's boxing. Middleweights."

"Isn't it odd how everything looks so much better in color?"

I was informed it was black and white. Everything is subjective. It looked like color to me.

Two more quick belts and I was out of money. One more, on the house, and I was suddenly out on the street, my rackets clattering on the sidewalk behind me, and somebody hollering at me to get out and stay out or my ass would be thrown in jail. I must have popped somebody but had no memory of who or why. These things happen when you are under match pressure.

Feeling kind of woozy, I made my way back to the stadium, argued with the ticket taker about getting in—it is easy enough to get out, but murder to get back in—and he called the USLTA prexy, who recognized me, and soon enough I was strolling down the primrose path toward the marquee and center court.

My hands were all scratched from falling into hedges and on the gravel and possibly on the sidewalk, and no man ever suffered so from thirst. Quick inventory: Rackets, shoes, pants buttoned, shirt on right-side out; they furnish the balls. . . . Well-wishers walking by, saying, "Hi, Charlie." "Going to sink the *Bismarck,* Mr. G.?" "You'll need this" —handing me a racket.

Walking through the marquee I fell down three times. Then, squinting out into the boiling sun, confronting dozing linespeople, a harried umpire, TV cameramen, the press with pencils poised, Forester hoisting his cup high in salud; and Heffernan in a dark business suit, all set to freeload at the subsequent banquet (no matter who won).

I stood there in a kind of soporific state, waiting for the umpire to introduce the principals and then holler, "Play ball!" so we could get the ghastly (for him and the Hapsburgs) struggle underway. If this thing goes to three sets, I am going to be in trouble, I thought.

"Hey, Forester!" I called, *sotto voce.*

He shook his head as though to say, "No more juice now, Charlie."

"Not that!" I assured him. "Clue me. Is this a five- or three-setter?"

He held up a bunch of fingers in his free hand. More than three, so I had to assume it was a five-setter. My God, I thought, I would rather be digging ditches among the mosquitoes on Devil's Island than play five sets in this heat. Because I was truly sweating. The racket would keep flying out of my hand. . . . Handkerchief! My God, had I brought my rackets but forgotten my handkerchief? I searched for it frantically. Ah! The one given me by Lady Vanderventer on the occasion of my serving as corespondent when she wished to divorce the duke. I had chills, along with the heat stroke.

I blew my nose in it.

That is the last I remember.

Later, at the banquet—a merry scene—Forester and I were toasting one another and absent friends in the various wassail bowls, one of which was my winner's trophy; and me being interviewed by the press and TV, when not being besought for autographs by aspiring lady tennis players and jaded members of the Jet Set.

"Hey, kookie!" Forester called over the din. He leaned toward me with a conspiratorial leer, indicating he wanted to tell me something confidential. "You figured out why Zammer defaulted, didn't you?"

I had not the vaguest, and so informed him.

"Gib! Gib! Gib!" from a bunch of newspaper reporters, sportsmen, and notables deep in their cups. Probably won ten million bucks by betting the right way, the Gibson way.

I waved acknowledgment. "You got me curious, Billy," I said, leaning over. "Because it would have been touch-and-go, me never having downed that much hootch before, especially before the Nationals. I needed a seeing-eye dog to find the court." And I told him as many of my adventures since departing the locker room as I could remember.

"That is a Mafia hangout," he intoned solemnly. "You were lucky to have escaped being kidnapped." I made a deprecatory response that brought sly smiles to all those within earshot. I had just been crowned champion for the fourth or fifth time and a well-deserved triumph does wonders for one's threshold of tolerance.

"But this is the thing!" He was forced to shout, for the ribaldry was getting out of hand, with tennis jokes being exchanged, my style being analyzed and compared with those of Tilden, Washer, Rutledge, van Ryn (a painter in his spare time), and other hall-of-famers, and the freeloaders freeloading with fast refills from the waiters.

"It was Sophie won it for you!"

"Who?"

"Sophie!"

Forester took a deep breath. "Just before she came to see us, she had already visited Zammer. Absolutely slaughtered him!"

"Far out!" I exclaimed, dipping my glass into the punch bowl, which somebody had the sense to fill with gin, not some grape juice they call champagne.

"Yeah. He was so exhausted from her ministrations, and I suppose some of his own—for he is a red-blooded young man—that he just couldn't make it out of the visiting players' locker room. Fell flat on his face—not that you weren't pretty close yourself, Charlie."

"I must have gone down ten times on the way to the arena that I remember. But, by God, thanks to American ingenuity and resourcefulness and the fact that we got two oceans between us, I got up every time and whupped him good."

"Anyway," he said—graciously, for him—standing up (and the room rose to a man) and raising his paper cup, "here's to the new American champion!" He toasted, hawked, spat, and made horrible grimaces, buckling over and hacking.

I rose and acknowledged the toast with one of my own, saying to myself: Stay cool, Charlie. Don't bawl. It looks bad in the papers—they'll call it a crying jag. Your enemies can use it against you. You are overwrought from all this celebration and adulation and the courage you pulled out from somewhere down deep within you to guts it out in that third—or fifth—set.

I gave credit to all the little people who had helped so much: The ball girls who handed me the particular ball I wanted for a particular point; the hard-working grounds keepers, who spent so much time straightening out the lines laid down by other groundskeepers.

Somebody was tugging hard at my sleeve. It was Forester,

who looked as if he had been giving himself a shampoo from one of the wassail bowls. (It turned out that one of the playful lady sportswriters, having set her cap for him, he being doubles champion and all—thanks to you-know-who, who would have won it partnered by a cigar-store Indian—had dumped a tankard of beer over his head and rubbed a raw egg in it. So I was not far wrong.)

"Listen, mon," he said, continuing to tug. "You won this thing by *default.* There were no ball girls or groundskeepers or lectures from the umpire on your conduct and sudden rages. If you had spent ten more minutes in that Mafia bar, we would be hailing *him* as the new champ. And you know who you could thank for it?"

"Who?" I said, trying to remember who "him" was. "First one today," and amid scattered cheers I downed a big slug.

"Sophie."

The name rang kind of a bell. Then the president of the IFLTA (or whatever they call it now) rose to his feet, picked up a knife by the wrong end and rapped imperiously on a glass, shattering it.

"Whoops!" he said amid general laughter.

"I hope I am not being charged for all this," I said to Forester in an aside.

He gave me a quick forget-it gesture and I gave him the Balkan salute.

"How about our having a dance with the king and queen of tennis?" the president hollered jovially. The applause was deafening. "Gib! Gib! Gib!" "Baranislava! Baranislava! Baranislava!"

"Who the hell is that?" I screamed in alarm at Forester over the bedlam. "Do they mean Balaklava? Are we at war with the Turks?" I looked around fearfully. "Because I've already done my bit."

"That's Sophie!" he shouted back. "The lady champ! You've got to dance with her! It's a tradition!"

Him telling *me* about tradition.

The orchestra (was I paying for it?) struck up a waltz and Forester and I had the same shocking thought in the same instant of time.

"My God! Sophie!"

Naked in a locker in the men's locker room.

"Well, at least she's got a quart bottle of hooch in there to keep her warm," Forester shouted over the bedlam and brouhaha that always characterizes the climax of these triumphal banquets.

We fell on one another's shoulders, laughing, laugh-crying, and in general carrying on.

That was the beginning of my affair with Sophie.

13

The Greatest Shot in Tennis History

People with an interest in sports, particularly those involved with feats that get into the record books, continually ask me what was the greatest tennis shot I ever saw.

A great many of my own would qualify for the semifinals in that department: A smash I hit against Don on an iceberg that never came up because it got stuck on a projecting icicle; a backhand I hit against that kid who uses two hands on his forehand. I guess you have noticed that between points he blows on his right hand. That is because he made the mistake of charging up to the net against me at La Costa behind a shot I could get set on.

I really socked this baby and it tore down the line and he cut it off—or tried to. The ball ripped the racket out of his hands and sent it flying twenty feet beyond the baseline. The strings lay there smoking on the ground and part of the frame was beginning to melt. I guess it was history's most applauded tennis shot.

He had been screaming at the umpire and linesmen that he wanted to default when he saw who his opponent was in the final. "I would *gladly* give up my fifty thousand dollars," he kept yelling to the officials before the match and on the changes of court. *"Gladly!"* But he had had to post a bond and they would not let him out of it. I should mention here that the prize was one hundred and fifty thousand dollars to the winner and fifty thousand dollars to the loser—so you can see how his mind was working.

After the shot, which I think made it 3-1 for me in the first set—I always warm up slowly—there was a thunderous ovation for about ten minutes, until the ushers had to turn the sprinkler hoses on the frantic spectators to cool them off so we could resume play. I heard that people all over Southern California kicked in their television sets, they were so delighted with this screaming backhand. A lot of viewers had to go to local bars to catch the rest of the match and watch the kid duck whenever I wound up on the left side. Fortunately, he had thought to bring an extra racket. The consumption of alcohol went up 12 percent in Southern California because of that particular match for the Far West championship, a lot of toasts being hoisted to that backhand. It was hit flat, with a touch of sidespin and a little topspin. That 12 percent figure is in *The Guinness Book of Records* under "The Most Remarkables," talking about establishing records. Some enterprising manufacturers were considering making a machine, like that one in the old days, when saloon patrons could box John L. Sullivan or Jack Dempsey—"Can you return Mr. G's backhand?"—three for a dime—but there were the usual royalty arguments and it never panned out.

Then there were *all* my shots against Zammer in Baden-Baden, supposedly the most one-sided match ever played on the international circuit. The only point that was not a placement was his double-fault at match point, which was purposeful, you may be sure. It was one time when the loser left the field more jubilant than the man who crushed him.

There was also a smash I hit against Kozeluh in Berne that struck the court surface so hard it caused an avalanche. We were playing on canvas stretched over Lake Geneva, which happened to be frozen solid (I have played on lakes and streams that were not frozen solid and, believe me, wading in ice water up to your chin after a crosscourt drop, the racket held over your head like an infantryman's rifle, is one of the tough retrieves of all time), and the ball hit what is called a fault. "Fault" is an earthquake term, meaning there is a fissure somewhere and the earth is constantly shifting in that area. This one moved about eighteen inches after I hit on top of it. Two inches gives you a seismic reading of six Beauforts on the Kroner scale, and San Francisco in 1903 only had a 1.5 reading.

Anyway, the match had to be postponed for eleven years because of some digging that had to be done to locate the court, and the fact that canvas was discovered by archeologists so many layers below the surface changed their thinking about Piltdown man—"My God, they had circuses in those days!" one of them remarked, and gave this Stone Age creature a lot more credit than he deserved.

I wrote the society a note, calmly explaining what happened, fended off a lawsuit, and the copies of their monograph were collected and burned. Six–four, six–one, forty-eight, forty-six, the last set a lot closer than the score indicates. Kozeluh had been taking secret lessons for eleven years, to explain his good showing.

But curiously enough, two of the greatest shots I ever saw occurred during the play of the same point. I hit a lob and Heffernan returned a lob. Perhaps my next shot should be included in this listing, making three in all.

Here was the situation:

The mixed doubles final of the International All-Comers Open at Wimbledon. Teddy Heffernan, U.S.N.R., O.B.E., and Laura Kingsley, the North Country champion, versus Sophie and myself.

The queen was there in her box, along with assorted dukes, earls, viscounts, baronets, baronesses, and cabinet officials. Tiaras and top hats were everywhere because this was the social event of the season and England was interested in selling our fifty destroyers back, "as is." And Heffernan, of course, had a lot of clout with the War Department.

Forester was there with a big delegation of butter-and-egg men from the Midwest, who were going to buy a distillery in Aberdeen and set him up as chairman and chief taster, a job for which he was admirably qualified. A noisy bunch of Teddy Boys were present, making eyes at all the cute ball girls, all in Tingaling costumes that dazzled the senses, and not paying much attention to the match except to hurl incomprehensible North Country obscenities at me whenever I was about to serve.

I should mention that, though I have won a score of international mixed doubles trophies with about ten different partners, I am not the most patient man in the world in the heat of competition, though God knows I am charming in a lounge or out in society.

Our side of the court would be in a constant squabble over strategy if it were not for the fact that I do not encourage fruitless talking. "Righto!" "Yours!" "Mine!" "Ouch!" (you will see why) and (to linespersons) "How in hell can you call that ball good? Look at the damn mark!" are about the only sounds my partner is allowed to make. And if she hollers "Yours!" she damn well better get off the court for awhile, because I am going to go after the ball if I have to knock her over and the umpire and three ball girls to get it.

If my partner balks at my instructions, *whacko!* She gets it with the racket or, if playing net on my serve, with a fast first delivery, hit flat with a little underspin, right to the buttocks so she can't sit down for a week.

One time, after a hard quarterfinal in Bristol, I took a tram to Tingaling's office and told him point-blank, "If you ever again put padding in those bloody ladies' tennis costumes, I am going to tear your factory apart! You damn near lost me the match!" He knew blasted well what I was talking about and my partner and I breezed through the semis and finals and, as she suspected, she could not sit down for a week. But the trophy was up on a mantel anyway, so who needed to sit down?

The score in this epic final match against Heffernan & Co. was 6-4 for us, 3-6 for them (the first set of any kind I had lost in five years except for lunch money) and 4-5 in the third, with 30-all in points, when one of the most sensational exchanges in tennis history took place.

Heffernan was about to serve to Sophie. I positioned her where she could at least make a blind stab at the ball. Laura (Heffernan's partner) was twirling her racket at the net, catlike, ready to pounce on Sophie's return.

Heffernan coiled and uncoiled, putting about three kinds of spin on the ball. Sophie lunged and poked it back. Heffernan moved in on his sea legs and sent a vicious forehand volley to Sophie's feet. She covered her eyes and I concluded that she could not possibly hit the ball back, so I rushed to my right and half-volleyed it off her shoetops. Laura reared back and smashed to the corner I had just vacated, but I was already on my way back there. After raising a mountain of chalk, the ball descended about thirty feet beyond the baseline.

With my back against the stands, dodging globs of debris hurled at me by the Teddy Boys and a few disgruntled earls, who know me as a popular corespondent, I hit one of the great lobs of all time.

As it soared high in the air I saw there was no possible way that Heffernan or Laura could return it, for it would surely bounce clear out of the stadium and I was thinking about how to play the next point and what instructions to give Sophie in the next game. However, I soon learned it was always dangerous to assume anything when pitted against a doubles team such as that of Heffernan and Laura.

To my utter surprise, Laura dashed over to a box near their baseline, borrowed a key from a uniformed attendant, rushed to a gate in the fence behind the court and flung it open. Heffernan rocketed out like a sprinter and ran about sixty yards. There was no time for him to turn and hit the ball, so he whacked it back over his left shoulder, making one of the greatest shots under pressure I have ever seen. Laura held the gate open for him so he could come back in. He was puffing.

Then I tried to follow the flight of the ball, shading my eyes. His lob was even higher than mine was and I knew, from the way he hit it, it was going to carry left-to-right spin. Up, up, and up it went. I imagine windows were slammed up (or down) all over eastern England.

"Sophie," I said quietly. "I want you to casually get off the court. Buy a ticket or sit in the stands or something. Because when this sonofabitch comes down I am going to need some room to maneuver."

She pouted. "If I'm your partner, I should stay on the court with you," she objected.

"No!" I was firm. "This is going to be one tough shot. Even for me—and you know I am very fast."

"Not with a buck," she said with a little snicker.

"Maybe we'd better trade rackets," I said, in no mood to bandy insults. "Yours has looser strings than mine and I've got to be extremely careful with a touch shot I plan to use and make that damn Laura trip over her feet. This is a critical point."

Reluctantly she handed me her racket. I held the strings to my ear and zinged them, which is how us experts tell how tight the gut is strung. C above middle C. Four notes lower than "Unquenchable," the racket I was using.

"It will have to do," I said, giving her my racket. "Be careful with it. Hit everything on the throat." It was a kind of joke, and those within hearing slapped their thighs and roared with laughter.

The ball had by now reached the zenith of its flight, enabling me to make some quick triangulations, or whatever you call them. It looked like it was going to land about halfway between the net and the rear serviceline on the right; after which, considering its spin and trajectory, its innards affected by its brush with the stratosphere with the result that its internal pressure would be up, plus the effect of gravity and the earth's rotation, it would probably bounce far to the right—landing, perhaps, a half mile from the stadium.

With the ball slowly arcing downward toward the ground, I made a wild dash out of the stadium. I heard the roar of the crowd as it bounced just inside the baseline and sliced up and out over the gaping spectators. I fought my way through hostile crowds, brushed off autograph seekers and finally arrived at a point near Leicester Square where I estimated the ball would come down.

I had miscalculated my position by fifty yards, but valiantly pursued the ball behind a friendly mounted policeman, leaped high in the air, frightening a whole flock of albatrosses into scattering, and swatted the ball.

It was a half-smash, half-lob—that is, a smash with a high trajectory to get over Nelson's statue. It hit the top edge of the net, barely trickled over into the forecourt, bouncing twice at Laura's feet just as Heffernan, to get himself off the hook, hollered loud enough for them to hear him in Calais, "Yours! You take it!"

"Advantage Mr. G.," intoned the umpire, a little shaken by all that had occurred.

But Heffernan is not the best sport in the world. He seized the ball from a ball girl and ran to the umpire's chair with it.

"This," he said through clenched teeth, "is not the ball I served." The umpire gave him a glance of aristocratic apathy.

I was on my way to the stadium in one of those crazy, tilting three-decker buses, meanwhile, but soon caught up with events.

"The ball I served," Heffernan asserted, "was a Wilson-Fulbright with three shields on it and the initials HRHS. It was colored green to match the grass and the background. And this happens to be a Wilkins-Masterfield, with twelve fleurs-de-lis on it and the initials KLIJ, as any fool can plainly see. Besides which it is seamless, hisses when you squeeze it, and is bright orange." He made it hiss. "Something funny is going on."

By that time I had arrived and sprinted past the ticket taker before he could demand a ticket and was confronting my archfoe.

"Heffernan," I told him. "You are a fool. You set two

records today. One for an outstanding piece of gamesmanship when you poured ketchup over three simulated rackets I placed out as a trap for you; and once when you hit the world's highest lob—higher than the one I hit in Denver, even when you consider I hit it from a point already five thousand feet above sea level. . . . If you want to play the point over, that lob is going to be disallowed and you will be relegated to ignominy in all the best gentlemen's clubs in the Western world.''

He spat on the turf. "Take the damn point," he said dourly. "Gimme the damn balls," he ordered one of the cutie-pie ball girls and made ready to serve.

You probably heard the story about Bill Tilden at one time in his career getting mad at the umpire, the crowd, and his opponent and picking up four tennis balls in his left hand and serving four fast aces. I am sure that Heffernan heard it, because that is what he did—at least he picked up four Wilson-Fulbrights and got set to serve in the ad court to me.

But the maestro has a trick or two up his sleeve. "Sophie," I called, as Heffernan began his interminable bouncing to put my nerves on edge. (I knew he would not serve before forty-nine, for that is supposed to be his lucky number. He is from Dallas, if that is any explanation.)

"Come over here."

She came over, a puzzled look on her face. "Stand in the center of the service court." A buzz went through the stands, and cleaning women dropped their buckets all over Soho. "What's he up to? What sort of trick is this?" Rulebooks came out.

Heffernan was so busy with his bounces and counting he did not notice the new arrangement, which I may call the Czechoslovak Receiving Formation. It is perfectly legal, but rare. If the serve hits the other party in the box, it is the serving team's point; and once the serve is returned, the box is well covered but the rest of the court isn't. So there are disadvantages as well as advantages.

The advantage was that when Heffernan got through his bounces and looked up and saw Sophie confronting him close to the net and me swaying catlike behind her, he blinked, thinking he had drunk too much warm ale the night before, made his toss and swung, and the ball skimmed by Laura's head so close that she turned in anger and flung her racket at him. The ball, incidentally, missed Sophie by a good two feet and was pronounced a fault by a linesperson of indeterminate sex.

Time was called while Heffernan argued that he should get two serves because his rhythm was interrupted. His rhythm was interrupted, actually, for twenty minutes while he argued and Laura fetched and tuned her racket. The umpire refused his demand and, somewhat deflated, Heffernan started bouncing for his second serve.

It was an important point—the match and championship for us, on the one hand, and a respite and maybe regained confidence for them, on the other. Sophie was swaying one way, close to the net, and I was swaying the other, about ten yards behind her. The toss. The back-scratch. The forward move. The arm upraised. The grunt. The ball struck. But—one of the ball girls had put gum or glue on it or something, out of vindictiveness at Heffernan's lack of manners, and the ball stuck to the strings.

He stared at it. Laura turned, wondering what in hell the problem was—even Heffernan should not be taking that long to serve. She instantly realized what had happened.

"Run up to the net!" she cried. "Throw the racket down in the service court! But don't lean over the net!"

"Whoa!" I said, moving forward. "That is a foot-fault."

"No, it isn't," said Laura. "Because the ball already made contact with the racket and now he can do anything he wants with it."

"Ruling!" Heffernan pleaded to the umpire, filled with anxiety, keeping his feet back of the line. Rulebooks came out, phone calls were made to the *Times*—both of London and New York, to Lloyd's of London, to the West Side Tennis Club, to Jack Kramer.

"For God's sake, Teddy, don't let that ball fall off the racket!" Laura screamed at him, when it seemed he had kind of dozed off while standing there. Meanwhile, I had to kind of protect the ad court in case of an unfavorable ruling, but I told Sophie to sit down by the centerpost.

In a few moments answers to the query came in from all over the globe. "Serve is good if it lands in box." "Foot-fault if he steps beyond the baseline." "Play a let"—from Henry Kissinger. "Heffernan's point"—from the Secretary of the Navy. "Watch out how you treat my little girl"—from Laura's mother. "Bond's of London has no record of your having a charge account"—from Her Royal Majesty. "Ball is automatically a fault"—from my bookmaker, whom the umpire happened to be into for two thousand pounds.

The umpire signaled the rear service court linesman.

"Out!" he cried, gesturing with his thumb.

"Out!" the umpire echoed, making ready to descend from his chair and head for the escape tunnel. "Game, set, match, and tournament to Mr. G. and Sophia Baranislava. . . . Well-played, ladies and gentlemen. . . . Good afternoon." And he disappeared like a shot.

I leapt over the net to offer congratulations to our opponents on the competition they furnished, thanked the ball girls for their services, Heffernan for *his* service (kind of half-smiling) and Laura for her screaming, which made me appreciate the little woman back home. Then I thanked Sophie for her support and joined Forester in the stands, where one helluva party was going on in Section E.

That is the tale of Heffernan's Lob.

14

Surfaces and Subsurfaces

A good hustler has to be able to play spectacularly on every type of surface. The variation is considerable—far more than that of the world's golf courses. On some surfaces the bounce is high; on some, low. On others the ball never comes up at all. Some are tough on the feet, on some you sink to your knees; on others, your timing is upset because of wandering alligators and cayugas (a different species of alligator).

I myself have played on dung in India; anthills in Australia (where you better wear shoes if you don't want to get nipped to death); on diamond fields in South Africa; on dough in Switzerland (some of it my own); on broken glass in a Japanese prison camp; slobbering through a rice paddy with a floating net near Seoul, Korea (thank God I did not have to furnish the balls, for they get mighty soggy); on sticky asphalt on a rooftop in New York's East Side, when it was 118° in the shade; on a quickly fabricated court on Fifth Avenue, made out of supermarket cartons, when I once had to put on an impromptu exhibition for Huntington Hartford. And so on.

There are two surfaces, though, that remain most vivid in memory. The first was on an iceberg, under dramatic circumstances.

It was during the influx of England by United States troops, prior to the invasion of the Continent. I was on the lead ship of the convoy, with a bunch of generals and admirals aboard—a dangerous and uncomfortable trip for some, though I weathered it pretty good.

At one point, off the coast of Labrador, the pilot shouted through the PA to the captain, "Here comes an iceberg!"

Whereupon everybody aboard put on their Mae Wests —*ah-ooga! ah-ooga!*—and started running around upstairs and downstairs, the way sailors and some soldiers do when there is a so-called emergency.

I was calmly reading Keats in a deck chair on the boat deck at the time.

The captain shouted back through his megaphone, "Where's the iceberg? I don't see no iceberg!"

"Naturally you can't see it," replied the pilot. "Because it is nine-tenths under water. That is simple physics."

"How come you can see the one-tenth and I can't?" hollered the captain.

"Because I am up here, dummy, and you are down there. If you weren't so interested in recouping your losses at dice with these sharpies, you would know what is happening on this boat."

Meanwhile, the soldiers and sailors on board were crowding into one another, pushing, shoving—"Battle stations!"—every soldier equipped to the nines (it wasn't like Verdun, when we went over the top with nothing but picture postcards of Montmartre in our hands to earn the goodwill of the Jerries), including a BAR; a bandolier of hand grenades; a copy of a booklet I once wrote called *How to Get Along on Fifty Yen a Day in the Ginza* (I admit this was the wrong theater for it, but I was not in charge of distribution; anyway, it may have fooled hell out of enemy intelligence); a chocolate bar (when there were *really* chocolate bars, not the prepackaged nonsense they sell now for a quarter); a set of crooked dice; an obsolete gas mask that God forbid the Germans should ever put to the test; a picture of John Wayne in the hip pocket for inspiration; an extra helmet to cook in; a pair of silk stockings—made by our friends the Japanese—in case the invasion and drive to Berlin turned out successful and some cutie fraulein was allergic to chocolate; a small card that said, "Your right hand is the hand you salute with"; a toupee, in case some of them should be pressed into service as double agents.

You can see they were pretty well loaded down, with nothing to do during the long journey but gripe and gamble and stand in line for the head and then stand in line for chow.

So when the captain asked me to play an exhibition tennis match on the iceberg to raise the spirits of the men, I consented, with reservations.

"The only problem is," I told him, "it is not going to be very exciting for the boys to see me bat balls against a chunk of floating ice, particularly since the balls are white and the ice is white"—the balls were white in those benighted days—"so it might—"

"Too bad we couldn't find a pink iceberg for you," he interrupted kind of dourly, not knowing how close he came to earning his purple heart right on the spot.

"It might be better, show-businesswise, as it were, if you could dig up some kind of opponent for me."

He gave me the vacuous look that must have frightened dozens of admirals.

"Who is on board?" I pursued. "Riggs, Kovacs, Heffernan, Kozeluh, the Gottliebs, Nogrady, Hartford, Parker, Grant? Because I do not want to hit with some goddam kid who isn't ranked between one and ten internationally. What I am getting at is that the men deserve to see some kind of reasonably dramatic exhibition.

"I confess," I added, *sotto voce,* "I have never played on an iceberg before. Especially with wolfpacks chasing up and down the North Atlantic trying to intimidate war correspondents, Red Cross girls, and pacifists drafted against their will. So if we make this arrangement, you've got to find what I consider a worthy opponent. A *name* player."

"Well, for Chrisakes, Charlie," the captain protested.

"When we loaded up this boat, or ship as they call it, we were not thinking of packing it with Class A tennis players! We wanted to fill it with GIs so they could undertake an invasion and save Belgium from the Hun."

"Well, that is your tough luck," I replied with a shrug, reopening my Keats. "I am not going to play some bum, even if it is on an iceberg and it's necessary to keep the GIs from taking over your ship." There was a sudden banging of messkits on the ship's left side. "If you can't drum up a worthwhile opponent, the deal is off."

He looked shocked. "What deal?"

"Well, you don't think I am going to play for *nothing,* do you? There should at least be a side bet on the match. You take my prospective opponent; I bet on me. Eight to five."

He looked suspicious. "Like how much?"

"How about twelve big ones?"

He considered it. "Done and done," he said, clasping my hand in a firm "brothers' grip" and trying to twist my thumb off. That is the way gentlemen's agreements are made.

So who do they find on board but the Old Redhead.

"What the hell are you doing here, Don boy?" I asked.

"I'm an artillery captain," he said, showing off his bars and crossed cannons. "I'm involved in this invasion bit."

"Who else is aboard?" I asked him. "Kramer, Parker—any Austrylians?" I chuckled.

"I doubt it," he said. "They've got their own troubles." He nodded to the west, the short way round.

The ship took a roll and a pitch as a torpedo whizzed by. "One thing, Don boy," I said, "dodging torpedoes isn't so bad, but if there's an air attack—pom-pom-pom!—it's going to be rough on the old concentration." There was a great jangling of bells as the captain ordered a hard right rudder—at about the time the torpedo had squirreled up a Labrador beach and sunk some cod fisherman's outhouse.

"It looks like it is you and me, Donno, on this here now iceberg."

"I hope these subs don't blow the ship out of the water, meanwhile," he said with a worried look. "Because that could be embarrassing—stranded on an iceberg with no ship to go back to."

"Maybe we could make a fire by rubbing two Wilsons together," I suggested with a certain amount of levity to relieve the tension. Those crewmen within hearing doubled over with laughter when they realized I was not serious.

Pretty soon we were close enough to the iceberg—a huge, frosty looking, marble white object shaped something like a mesa, with icicles hanging down like earrings and gently rocking in the tides of the Humboldt Current.

A bosun stood on the bow and harpooned the thing to hold it steady and a couple of deckhands hurled the ship's anchor onto it to make it fast. A few minutes later Don appeared, wearing a parka, mountain-climbing shoes and a blue-and-white warm-up suit. I myself was garbed in ski pants, mukluks with spikes, four sweaters, mittens attached to each other with a string, a red-and-white warm-up suit and a Cossack hat in the event some MIGs might be flying over.

With some difficulty we jumped onto the thing and caught our balance. A mile-a-minute wind was blowing, whipping ice spars past us and at us, tearing rents in our clothing. It was going to be tough to keep the ball in play, I reflected.

A bunch of Seabees leapt onto the berg, shooed away some curious seals and sea lions from the flattest expanse they could find—and then one of them came running toward Don and me over a kind of rise—arroyo, I think they call them in Norwegian.

"Hey!" he hollered to us, cupping his hands, "the damn court is already taken!"

"Can't be," I said sternly. "Anyway, a match like this takes precedence over any—"

Then I realized he must be kidding. When the war was over we would have a drink together, I mused. Dutch.

In the meantime, the Seabees had pounded belaying pins into the ice and strung up a bunch of hammocks to serve as a net. Others painted black lines onto the surface so we could tell whether a ball landed in or out.

When this was done, Don and I started rallying, interrupted by seals and narwhals who thought we were hitting balls for their amusement and seemed to be eager to get jobs at Barnum & Bailey. The crew quickly scrambled up the shrouds and ratlines, or whatever they have on ships that go by propeller, so they could witness the epic event.

Despite the howling wind, the match progressed uneventfully, each of us losing serve because no sooner did you release the ball than a sharp blast blew it due east. And then I noticed the berg was drifting against the current.

Many people believe that all rivers have to flow south, because when you look at them on maps, they would otherwise have to flow *up*. And water, whatever its other characteristics, cannot flow *up*. Not for long, anyway. Yet here was this ice palace fighting against the current, against all natural laws.

I pulled Don up to the net with a backspin drop shot and while he was scooping it up at the cost of the frame and strings on his racket, I said to him, "This iceberg is moving funny."

"Yeah," he said cynically, convinced I was trying to distract him. "And Albania has come into the war on the side of the Turks."

"The next time you serve," I advised him, "look at the ripples."

So he did, and shortly thereafter drew me to the net with a drop shot which I put away after tripping over a basking dugong.

"You're right," he acknowledged. "There's a propeller at the south end!" A moment later he said, "There's a cook with the kaiserin cross flinging sauerbraten out of a hidden porthole!"

"It is a German raider, like the *Emden* in World War I!" I asserted. "What a fiendish device!"

"What do you suppose we ought to do?" he inquired.

"We have three choices. Capture it; sink it; melt it."

I forget what the captain finally ordered. Maybe there was a fourth alternative, like breaking it up into ice cubes for chilled bourbons-and-water. All I know is, Don never completed the set and managed to stiff me out of twelve big ones.

Another odd surface I played on was metal. You may say, well, that is not so unusual: If they can make courts of rubber, they can make them out of metal.

But this metal was on the foredeck of a heaving, yawing, pitching cruiser off Saipan—and part of the time it was under attack by Kamikazes. Those are factors that would disturb anyone's concentration.

Here is how the match came about:

I had volunteered to help break the Japanese code in 1943 and was being transported by cruiser, along with some generals and admirals and boxes of Spam, to the island of Truk—from which I would take a chartered plane to Naha, Okinawa. (That island was still in the hands of the Japanese, but it was figured, by Washington and ASCAP, that the closer I got to the Japanese radio transmitters in Kyoto, the faster I would crack the code.)

Off Palau, my cover was broken by some sailor tennis fan who recognized me. "The maestro is on board!" The word buzzed around the ship. A lot of the generals and admirals with us came around to congratulate me on winning the Big Six four years in a row.

Then somebody said, at chow, "Isn't 'Heffernan' the name of the captain of this vessel?"

I jumped at the sound of the name. But it couldn't be Teddy Heffernan. He'd never had the guts to get into a rowboat, let alone guide a cruiser through enemy waters. Some research was done by a man named Halsey, who was headed for Melbourne, and he came up with the information that it was Heffernan, Theodore K., which had to be the one and only original Teddy Heffernan.

"Hey, wouldn't it be great," one of the generals suggested, "if the maestro here and Heffernan could play a three-setter?"

"My God, Mac," said one of the admirals. "He's got a whole convoy to nurse to Brisbane. That's a responsibility!"

"I was just noodling," the man said.

But the pressure was on. The sailors wanted to see it, about five thousand marines wanted to see it, all the passenger brass wanted to see it. When he was approached, Heffernan blanched as though he had the ague and made a thousand excuses, but finally acceded.

He called me to his cabin, all dressed up in gold braid to psych me out.

"Mr. G.," he said, "I think we have a face-to-face match up and confrontation here."

"I don't think 'match up' is the proper term. For, as I recollect, I don't believe you have taken a set off me in three years."

"Your recollection is notoriously faulty," he said with a sneer.

I pretended to be reluctant. Indeed, playing on the deck of a moving cruiser is something I had never done—and for all I knew, Heffernan did it regularly. He was (and is) that kind of sport.

We walked out onto the bridge, or whatever you call it. The wind was blowing up pretty good.

"What about a net?" I asked him. "I won't play without a net."

"Yeah, I got a net." He blew his pitchpipe and a bosun appeared as if by magic. "Bring out the net," he ordered.

"Roger, sir, or whatever it is they say in nautical lingo," said the bosun, saluting, and he ordered a huge crane to go up and bring down a whole bunch of naked girls in a huge fishnet.

"Jesus Christ, bosun," exclaimed Heffernan, stamping up and down the foredeck, with his hands behind his back. Turning, he shouted into the wind, "I don't mean that kind of net! Send them back up. I mean a *tennis* net."

"Tennis net? *Tennis* net? What are you, captain, sir, some kind of queer? Tennis is when you hit them pink little balls back and forth—" He hesitated, while Heffernan, with all the might of the Navy Department behind him, gave the bosun a freezing glare and the salt spray banged against his lips. "Oh, I get it, sir. You got Mr. G. aboard and you want to make an impression on all that goddam brass we're ferrying. . . . Right away, sir. I'll have the ship's carpenter make one up in a jiffy out of the enlisted men's tablecloth." He saluted smartly, squared his cap and shrieked orders into the wind.

In a few minutes he had a net strung up between a couple of capstans and binnacles on the foredeck. Heffernan broke open the ship's locker to bring out four rackets and two cans of balls. He gave me one of the rackets and we went downstairs, as best we could, to the foredeck.

The ship was pitching and yawing, for a nor'easter was behind us and every man jack in the audience, hanging over yardarms, and leaning down from foremasts, and posted everywhere else they have places to hang from on a ship bucking a wind of 8 Beauforts, had on his galoshes and raincoat, it was that nasty a day.

I took the port side of the net, because the ship was rolling in that direction and it was easier than trying to climb up to the starboard side. Heffernan hung onto the railing to keep from being swept overboard and yelled something at me.

"I can't hear you, Heffernan," I hollered back as a wave

caught me from the rear and sent me sliding to the net and the roll of the ship sent me sliding back. "We can't communicate vocally," I hollered to him. He nodded and sent his communications officer down to the cellar to bring up two signalmen with signal lights. "I'm glad you didn't order semaphore!" I shouted into the wind, "for when your signalman is horizontal to the deck a C looks like a T!"

He nodded as though he understood, but I know the wind beat back my words, for it was against me—a typical Heffernan trick. His signalman asked my signalman if I wanted to serve. I had him signal back "Negative."

It took quite a while to spell it out, because half the time he was so spun around by the waves that his blinking light was aimed at other ships in the convoy. Blinkers started flashing from all over the fleet. A lot of them said, "For God's sake, keep light discipline! We are in enemy waters."

And some waggish captain would have his signalman reply, "Jesus Christ, I thought we were on the Hudson, opposite Bear Mountain"—to the great delight of the seamen on the ship that received the signal.

"All right," I had my signalman notify Heffernan. "I will serve." I had noticed that the ship was about to take an immense roll, in my favor, as it were, because if you are serving downhill, as any fool must know, you have the advantage.

With some difficulty (because I was holding onto the railing with one hand), I made the toss (a low one on account of the gale blowing) and served.

"Fault!" came the signal.

"Fault, hell," my signal came back.

"Play two."

"That's better."

But by this time the ship had pitched and yawed and rolled so that I was virtually horizontal and the deck was at a 60 degree angle upwind of me, or whatever the naval parlance is. I thought I would wait for a more favorable moment.

The ship was about to take an immense roll
in my favor

"Serve, dammit. I am captain of this vessel."

I told my signalman, "Signal back, message not received, and if received, not understood."

"Grrrr," his signalman said.

But finally, with the both of us being resourceful players, we got the game under way, though the crew was kept hopping to prevent the balls from being washed overboard, especially when I smashed downhill. (Thank God they were his, or the Navy's.) One time the pilot shouted down to him, "We're listing! We're listing!"

"Don't you think I know it?" Heffernan cried. It was in the middle of a rally. "My goddam lobs are sailing out!"

The one thing that kept him in the game was that every time one of his shots was about to miss a line he would holler, "Come about!" to the helmsman, who would twist the steering wheel with all his might and the ship would make a sharp left turn—and the ball would land in.

On the other hand, the maestro is no dummy. After the captain had made several points this way, I discerned his strategy and, when it was to my advantage, I would yell, "Come about!" And, by God, the helmsman would do it.

The result of the match?

Well, with us zigzagging, the whole convoy had to zigzag, thinking it was a wolf pack of submarines or a flight of Kamikazes attacking. So, instead of going straight, we zigzagged all the way from Palau to Truk, adding about eighteen days to the trip, but only about four days to the war.

(*Six-four, five-three, in my favor when interrupted by a Kamikaze attack.* That is how it is in *Guinness.* Check it out.)

About the Author

Rex Lardner has written hundreds of magazine articles, most of them dealing humorously with various sports, and he also has to his credit fifteen published books, including *Downhill Lies and Other Falsehoods* (a recent Hawthorn hit), *The Great Golfers, Out of the Bunker and into the Trees, The Legendary Champions,* and the inimitable *The Underhanded Serve.*

When Lardner isn't seated at his typewriter, working away at an article or a new book, he can usually be found out on a tennis court belaboring some poor, unsuspecting opponent with his own special brand of clever shotmaking, combined with a generous sampling of psychological gambits.

He lives in Great Neck, New York, with his wife and three children.